BECAUSE I'M
RICHARD'S
SON

GREG FISH

CORBINFOSTER
PUBLISHING

I dedicate this book
to the loving memory of my parents,
Richard and Florence Fish.

- The Tennessee Stud -

Posted On Social Media, June 18, 2021.

"And there never was a hoss like the Tennessee Stuuuuuud." Dad would rare back and let the notes fly, all the while content in the knowledge that he was tormenting my soul with his singing. Dad certainly loved to sing, he loved those old songs, but he also loved to use his strong voice to get under my skin. Truth is, he was already under my skin, in my bones, knitted into my DNA, and painted on my soul. And what I wouldn't give to call him up for Father's Day and hear him cheerfully greet me with a, "Hey son! How's it goin'?" I'd even let him sing about that old Tennessee Stud if he wanted. Dad's voice has never gone away, and in fact, I hear it take rise in my own voice on occasion. There are moments when I realize I'm standing like dad, clearing my throat like he did, and even thinking thoughts that are surprisingly close to what he might be thinking if he were around today. Dad and I made disagreeing with each other an art form, but truth is, apples and trees have a way of living into old proverbs. "Hey son." Two words that I heard thousands of times, and I am certain they will be among the first words I hear when I cross over Jordan, as dad would have put it. There's an old song stuck in my head today thanks to dad. But there's also a rich legacy of love, hope, and character that is built into my being simply because I'm Richard's son. Happy Father's Day, dad. I love you.

ONE OF MY **FAVORITE PICTURES** WITH DAD. WOULD LOVE TO HAVE A RESHOOT, THOUGH. **TODAY.** I'D BE IN BETTER SHAPE. **DAD WOULD STILL BE HERE.** SOUNDS LIKE A WINNER TO ME.

1

– Half the Man –

If I can be half the man my dad was, I will have lived a good life.

I've repeated that phrase often throughout my days. It's always been a convenient way of admitting that I never measured up. I wasn't the man I thought I should be. Dad stood tall in my mind, thoughts, and recollections of home. I skirt the shadows of time in hopes that no one will notice that I'm a poor imposter of a man who, in my mind, has become legendary.

From the quiet, gently rolling hills of Southern Indiana, to the foothills of the Alleghenies, to the flat plains of Illinois, and into the yellow-hot summers of Texas, Richard Fish has been my companion as I've traveled this world. My father's voice guided me through my formative years, cried with me in profound loss, and still speaks from the distant shores of Jordan.

In the summer of my 56th year, I was welcomed into Texas with several months of consecutive triple-digit heated days. And for the first time in my adult life, I heeded the message that Richard Fish had long ago tried to inculcate into my resiliently resistant mind. My health was worth tending to, and my body was a garden that needed constant care. After shedding the pounds that had addled me with high blood pressure and low energy, I dared to return to those days following college, where I ran. Could I, at this point in my life, dare to run again? Richard Fish was there with me every step of the way.

"Son, this is a dream come true," dad said enthusiastically as I strapped on my sporty new Nike running shoes and prepared for my first run with dad. He had become a runner several years prior, and I had only gotten fatter through my college years.

"I read this book, *A Father-Son Run*, and I started dreaming about this day, son," dad said, barely masking his elation. "I always hoped the day would come when we could run together."

After graduation, I felt the sting of being alone. Oh, to be sure, I had a beautiful family and a wonderful group of friends at the Columbus, Indiana, Free Methodist Church. But I was overweight, depressed, and longing to find the right partner to walk with through the remainder of my days. I knew it was time to pay attention to my body's complaints about how I was treating it. And perhaps, along the way, I'd also find that love I was looking for.

But that first run was a death march for me. My youth was no match for dad's physical well-being. My feet slapped hard against the pavement and I often stopped to find my lost breath.

"It's OK, son, you'll get there." Dad jogged in place as I gasped and wheezed.

But then, this new challenge began to take shape. Dad and I fell into sync with each other on the road, and I felt my body grow stronger. We started to have conversations while we ran.

"Dad, what's it like to be so close to 50?"

"Well, son, I don't know what it's supposed to feel like, but I don't feel like it."

That made perfect sense.

Once I achieved the goal of keeping up with dad on the runs, a new challenge was needed. At the end of each run, dad would, in his words, "lay it on." He would speed up for the final stretch as I struggled to keep up. I struggled day after day. But then...

I knew we were about to the point on the trail where dad would lay it on. And instead of waiting, the day came when I put down the challenge. I felt my feet moving the pavement effortlessly, the wind graciously circling my face as I glided through the air. I knew what Clark Kent must've felt as he tossed his glasses aside and soared through the air as Superman. I could have been flying at that moment.

With Olympic-worthy form, I arrived at the finish point only to realize that dad, who was running with all of his might, was lagging well behind me. As he finally arrived at the car, he was laughing through the heavy breaths.

"Well, son, you finally did it. You beat the old man."

I never intended to beat the old man, and I could never best Richard Fish. And yet, in the summer of 1988, I found my wings.

Thirty-four years later, I was still running with dad. He left this earth for higher lands in 2013, but he was still with me, our hearts still beating to the same rhythm, our feet still touching the hem of Earth.

Dad was with me. I heard him when I cleared my throat, and I heard him when I laughed or sighed. I saw him when I held my chin in my hand with my fingers draping my cheek. And as I walked and occasionally dared to run the trails of Fort Worth, my dad was there praying along with me.

As dad entered his fifties, his knees demanded that he trade running for bicycling. I felt the same strain in my half-century knees as I occasionally dared to challenge the pavement in my baby blue Hoka Clifton 8s. But on the occasions that I decided to lay it on, dad was there with me.

Perhaps it's a DNA thing. Maybe it's the thickness of a lifetime of memories. Perhaps there's something more divine at play. But Richard Fish has been with me even through the years he has been gone. Or, maybe it's me that is gone, ambling my way toward the finish line.

As the breeze circled my face and the sweat gathered on my brow, I once again said, "Dad, if only I were half the man you were."

But there's a lot more to the story. There are rich, fragrant tales waiting to unfold. There are fish to be caught, lessons to be learned, gardens to tend, people to help, and more miles to run. And there are puzzles to resolve and questions to ponder that I've gained on this journey because I'm Richard's Son.

2

– Something Better Than Great –

I believe that good is better than great.

Many people have graciously told me that my dad, Richard Fish, was a great man. It feels disrespectful to disagree with anyone who says that. We deal casually with terms like greatness in our culture, readily handing out "Number One Dad" t-shirts and mugs to affirm someone's position in our hearts and minds. But my dad holds a place in my heart that exceeds greatness. He was good.

I fidgeted like a child, sitting in that over-stuffed office chair in my counselor's office.

I nervously dug fingernails beneath fingernails, aware of the billowing tissues all puffed out of the box, just waiting for me to succumb to the need for them. They sat on the table, beckoning me to break into tears and find comfort in their soft embrace. Why do counselors seem so intent on making you cry?

My eyes scanned the diplomas and certifications freckling the walls of that small office. Then, my gaze returned to the stoic but kind figure sitting there in a ready, open manner, waiting for me to unburden myself of the details that had brought me to that moment of existential crisis deep into the fifth decade of my life.

I had lost so much of myself, and the rivers of past years had worn off my edges, creating smooth, lifeless stones in my heart. Layers of grief, anxiety, and struggle had laid their heavy beds of sediment into my deepest reaches.

I was widowed and had just survived the overwhelmingly sad ending of a new relationship. I lived alone, hundreds of miles from family. A sense of failure and worthlessness had overtaken me.

It was 2020, in the months before the pandemic came and the world stopped turning. I was in a new section of my journey through life, in a place where the winds of discontent never stopped blowing. The familiar and comfortable parts of my life were being driven from my grasp like tumbleweeds, and I found myself trying to remember who I was. Not that the new was bad, it was just different and seemed to hold little concern for all the things past that had made me and shaped me. As a result, I felt like a stranger in my own skin as I tried to create a new life in Peoria, Illinois.

Wisely, the counselor declared it was time for me to reconnect with the core values of my life. He asked who I most admired. The answer came quickly. I most admired my dad. It felt like a trite, cliche answer, but it was right on the tip of my tongue.

I told of my dad's servant-heart. I mentioned his love for people. He was the hardest-working man I've ever known. That's a subjective evaluation, but I have met very few who have impressed me with their devotion to hard, labor-intensive work, like my dad. He was proficient at fixing cars, raising gardens, and catching fish. He was a man of God of biblical proportions. I can say that because men of Scripture also tended to be deeply flawed individuals who found strength in God to do things their nature would not allow.

While many people knew and attested to the greatness of my father, I knew the man behind the scenes. I knew things about him that brought him shame. I saw the secret inner workings of my father as much as I could without going inside his mind. He was a godly man of influence and character that bore the marks of many mistakes.

Still, the counselor seemed slightly startled to hear my final analysis of dad.

"He was good, not great. But I think that's better," I reasoned.

Head tilted and brows furrowed, he asked me to unpack that idea. Why would I say that good is better than great?

Greatness is a highly extolled virtue that we all find incredibly difficult and painful to live up to. I suspect my dad would have told you that he was not half the man his daddy was. I've often thought that if I could be half the man my dad was, I would do quite well. Greatness can make us feel like failures in the comparison bubble. Greatness is admirable, but it can feel unobtainable.

Though many people aspire to greatness, no matter how high they rise, the measuring stick can always be held higher. People of great wealth have difficulty believing they are rich; they often want more. There is never enough wealth to satisfy that kind of hunger.

However, goodness is something even the most under-resourced among us can achieve. Goodness is not measured by the standard of perfection; it always comes riddled with the pockmarks of life. Goodness is right and just and honorable and pleasing. The scales of goodness have only one tray, and goodness is measured only against itself. Either it is, or it isn't. Where greatness can typically find something greater, goodness is always good. You never hear of someone who is gooder or goodest.

That was my dad; good. And that is the only measure I find that I can live by. Trying to be great has driven me to points of anxiety and despair. Being good has always been a shoe that fits.

Good is better than great, though good itself resists that demarcation. Good is something we all can do. It's something we all can be. And good is something we all can live out. Good leaves a legacy of hope. Good shelters others with grace and mercy. Good always finishes the race well, even if not in first place. Good helps us find our way when we're lost. Good finds the wisest path to take. Good discovers our hope and brings it to light.

I had the divine honor of walking for a time with a man who was good. He was the compass pointing me to the true north, the Good Father.

I hold my dad up as a positive influence. But I'm careful not to raise him high on a pedestal. He didn't achieve anything in life that was unobtainable. We can live the same quality of life, and we can apply the same metrics to our journey no matter how different our journey may be. We all have the correct leavening of goodness already inside, waiting to rise.

Even though life has changed and upended me in ways I could have never predicted, I have found that I can be good. I'm sure you can as well.

Dad could instinctively look at an engine and know what was wrong with it. I struggle to find the clasp that releases the hood of the car.

Dad could touch metal and wood to dirt and stir it in such a way that plants would grow to impressive heights, produce uncommon bounties of vegetables, and look as spectacularly groomed as a fellow on his wedding day. I tend to let the weeds take my weak little plants if they want them that badly.

Dad could climb on top of the house with the ease of an acrobat reaching for the next trapeze, then chimney-sweep the flue with extraordinary precision just in time for winter's onset. I get a bit shaky on a step stool.

Dad could thread fishing lures on lines and calculate the right casting strength, wind speed, and water temperature, divided by the time of day and multiplied by the number of moons around Jupiter. He would then catch any unsuspecting fish that went sashaying through the water. I simply threw the line out and hoped for the best.

My dad and I were different. But I found my place.

There are seeds of his proficiencies in me, but they cross-pollinated with mom's buoyant sense of humor and quirky way of looking at life. Somehow I was always able to find the words to write and speak. I've never reached any form of greatness, but I suppose I have a goodness that has touched my spirit from time to time. I'm confident that the great things any man measures himself against can never entirely overshadow the simple good that nests in his soul. Dad lived a life of God-embedded, tragedy-defined, daily-breath-divined good things. Some might say my dad reached the heights of greatness. You and I know better. Greatness is too high and wide and deep. Goodness is right here among us.

I learned that because I'm Richard's son.

MOM & DAD
FROM SOMEWHERE IN TIME.

3

– The Legend of the Blind Horse –

Amid the deep-cut hollers and hills of Southern Indiana years ago, when the world was still black and white, an old man rode his blind horse into town every weekend. There, in that sleepy little village where the churches outnumbered the bars, the old man would tie the horse to a post and then enter one of the establishments where he could indulge his thirst for copious amounts of liquor. He would proceed to get lavishly, out-of-his-mind drunk.

At the end of the evening, patrons of the saloon would take the man, who had passed out on the floor, place him on the back of the old, blind horse, and free it from its tether.

Slowly, the horse would point its nose towards home and begin the laborious journey over the winding dirt roads of Jackson County, Indiana. The darkness of the night would be no challenge to that sightless, swayback nag as it walked the path through the hinterlands by some magical means knitted into the core of its being.

Eventually, the horse with the stupefied rider would successfully navigate the miles through the foothills and around the cricks to arrive safely home.

Legend has it that is how Blind Horse Holler got its name. It was thanks to an old horse that never lost its way and a wayward rider lost in a drunken haze.

———————————

Many years later, Blind Horse Holler was the homeplace of Ina Hanner, who married and tamed the soul of the wild, whiskey-drinking Glen Fish. He willingly laid aside the fiery elixirs in exchange for the privilege of drinking in life with the one he loved. Though it would always seem like Glen was the strong, iron-fisted one, Ina's fierceness could outmatch his. She, after all, was the one who could out-hunt her brothers when it came to shooting squirrels.

From the hills and hollers where they were born to the rural farmland of Bartholomew County, my Grandma and Grandpa Fish traveled the winding roads of life, often stumbling blindly by intuition alone, like that old blind horse. They persevered and, along the way, gave life to my father and his five siblings; Martha, Gloria, Jack, Richard, Jerry, and James.

———————————

Richard, a country boy, married Florence Foster, a strong-willed city girl from Indianapolis. They were lost on life's winding trails until a fateful meeting at church camp. Blind Horse Holler may be where this story begins, but it was in Clay City, Indiana, that this story finds form and function.

My sister, Stephanie, and I came out of that blessed union. As a boy, I was fascinated that though I was called Greg, I was the proud owner of a longer name: Gregory. There was a phase of life where I insisted upon being called by the full monicker. That day has long passed, and you can call me Greg.

I grew up enjoying fresh, homegrown vegetables, crispy fried chicken, sweet peach cobbler, pop-tarts, and Ho-hos. I knew the feel of a firm swat to my bottom when I was being contrary. I learned how to dig deep ditches with vigor and how to hoe delicately around tender, young, sprouting plants. I grew up to the feel of a scorching fire in a cast-iron stove on wintry nights when the Rook cards would come out and salty, bacon-grease popcorn was served in brown grocery store paper bags.

I've never lost the smell, taste, or feel of those memories. But I have sometimes lost my sense of direction.

Every Fourth of July, our family of four would make the pilgrimage to Blind Horse Holler for the family reunion.

The long journey into the depths of the hills and hollers was interminably long to my impatient, young soul. I couldn't understand why they didn't pave the roads. The dusty gravel was too far removed from modern-day byways for me to comprehend why such a thing could exist.

The old homeplace was a page out of history that seemed ill-fitted for those early 1980s. Uncle Eldon didn't even have indoor plumbing for most of the years I visited Blind Horse Holler. But that was OK with us kids. We looked forward to making full use of the outhouse. Something was compelling about that strange, smelly, hot wooden box to a child who didn't have to deal with one on a day-to-day basis. There was never any toilet paper in that old two-seater (did they ever fire up both seats simultaneously?). However, they must've done their shopping from the outhouse because there were always Sears and Roebuck catalogs stacked on the floor.

"Dad, why can't we get an outhouse?"

Dad would look back at me with a dumbfounded, "what brand of stupid are you, anyway?" sort of expression.

Uncle Eldon would draw water from the well and fill a large, shiny silver canister. It was the best-tasting, coldest water I've ever had.

While the family laid out a magnificent feast on the old flatbed, we kids would go wading and hunting crawdaddies in the crick. Crick is the correct word; the word creek is inadequate. The chilly water would tickle our ankles, and minnows would dance around our feet as we carefully measured each step on those slick, green rocks. The older kids would often sit, in their superiority, on the fallen tree that provided a natural bridge across the crick. We aspired to the day when we could move up the caste and assume our beloved spot on the old tree.

My grandma's brother, Uncle Eldon, seemed like the sweetest, kindest man that ever lived. His generous smile and gentle voice were magnetic to my heart. Spending time talking with him was a finer event than being in the presence of any president, king, or celebrity could ever be.

After we stuffed our bellies with meatloaf and fried chicken and lemonade and berry cobblers, we'd leave those hallowed grounds and find our way back over the blind horse's memorable trail lined with geode-filled cricks and tall, ancient trees.

I'm traveling that road right now in my heart.

Even though I never thought that I was much like my father, I find that in these years of his physical absence from my life, he still visits me. I hear him in my laugh, in the way I cough, in particular words I find myself saying, and in my desire to find my way closer to God. In a twist of life, dad and I have something curious in common; we both came to know what it is like to watch a wife die after 25 years of marriage. When mom died, dad had just turned 50. When Barbara died, I was about to turn 50.

As I sit tonight thinking about dad and how he painted and carved unique designs into my life, I once again reach for a memory to sustain me one more mile of this journey. I take in a deep breath, imagine him sitting here with me, and settle in for another long talk. I once considered his simple, country ways to be too imperfect for me. Now they seem like a bright light shining on my path.

———————

I've heard people say things like, "My best days are behind me." Or "I'm worthless. This world would be better off without me."

"I feel lost," some might say. "I need a sense of hope."

Others face the challenge of life's mysterious winding roads, saying, "I'm up for a new challenge! I'm ready to go for it."

A strong father has honed my survival skills. And thanks to his influence, I am firmly convinced that we all have access to a strong Father throughout our journey traversing the woods of life.

I'm not sure if the legend of Blind Horse Holler is true or not. Big stories have a way of growing out of small truths. But I do love the film that plays in the theatre of my mind; I love watching that old blind horse find its way down the same twisting, hilly roads that I recall from when we visited grandma's old homeplace. I hold tight to the lesson that there is a way home when we are at our lowest and most lost.

Think about this Psalm for a moment:

"Show me the right path, O Lord;
point out the road for me to follow.
Lead me by your truth and teach me,
for you are the God who saves me.
All day long I put my hope in you.
Remember, O Lord, your compassion and unfailing love,
which you have shown from long ages past.
Do not remember the rebellious sins of my youth.
Remember me in the light of your unfailing love,
for you are merciful, O Lord.

"The Lord is good and does what is right;
he shows the proper path to those who go astray.
He leads the humble in doing right,
teaching them his way.
The Lord leads with unfailing love and faithfulness
all who keep his covenant and obey his demands."
(Psalm 25:4-10, NLT)

What a wonderful way to find our sense of direction when we are lost, when we are ready to move, or when life has thrown another curve at us. It starts with our desire to find our way. SHOW ME. Show me the right path, the road to follow; this is the point at which we get our bearings straight.

Next, we express our willingness to move forward. LEAD ME. Teach me, show me, lead me, and I will follow; this is where we learn to trust the one who saves us and find that we have reason to hope.

Then, we pray to God, asking him to REMEMBER. Remember your compassion and love that never fails. After all, this is the stuff that truly inspires us. When we know we're loved, and that God has mercy on us despite our errors, we begin to figure out that we have reason to keep going.

Finally, we ask God to FORGET. "God, please forget the stinker I used to be." I find the word stinker fits quite a few of us.

There's something beautiful and divine about God's love and mercy. Even though we learn and grow from our past, and sometimes we have to live in the after-effect of our choices, something is enlightening about how God's mercy moves us forward. Mercy is the aha moment our hearts need to realize that God defines us by a different standard than the world does.

When you put it all together, it comes out in a simple prayer that I've formed:

"Father, SHOW ME the way...

LEAD ME, and I will follow...

REMEMBER your unfailing love...

FORGET my failure...

My hope is in you."

I hope that prayer will be helpful to you as you seek the words you need, as you seek the direction you've lost, and as you seek the hope your soul feeds on. I also hope these simple stories will inspire you to keep moving, unchain your pain, and embrace the power of our hope in Jesus. There's no other way I can tell this story. It's ingrained in me. It's part of my DNA.

It's who I am because I'm Richard's son.

THE BOY I
NEVER KNEW.

4
– I'll Show You Who's Boss. I'll Join the Army –

The Greyhound bus engine revved with road-ready determination as the dust on that 1950s-era road sifted through the midday air, covering those waving goodbye from the wood-plank departure area.

Dad looked back and saw a site that galvanized his soul. It was a Rockwell-style imprint of his parents, Glenn and Ina Fish, clutching each other tightly. As the dust and exhaust ungraciously circled the two, his mother wiped tears from her eyes and bowed her head.

―――――

"We were probably poor. But we never knew it then," dad would say.

Dad breathed deep into his thoughts as he stirred up beautiful memories of his post-depression era raising.

Grandpa was a hard-working man who instilled that ethic into each of his six children. Both love and the sternest of discipline were present at all times in the small but adequate house nestled amid the rural expanses just outside of Columbus, Indiana.

In a time when domestic televisions and radios were still in high demand, grandpa worked at Arvin's, a local manufacturer of quality electronics. And mufflers. And they churned out the odd car part as well. When Arvin's had paint to spare, the employees could take some home. One year, grandpa was given brown and dark yellow paint. He proudly announced to the family that they would paint the house chocolate and butterscotch.

Dad may have been among the last American generation to attend a one-room schoolhouse. He fondly recalled his teacher, who was compassionate yet ready to yield a sapling switch at a moment's notice. Teachers in that era were a ponderous combination of educators who knew how to apply the three R's and were quick to apply the swing of a stick when a student was judged unruly. It was an unspoken rule that if your behavior merited punishment at school, you would get it double at home.

The gravel and dirt road-dusted Indiana countryside bestowed a certain Huck Finn freedom upon a young boy. Dad and his brother Jack were as tight as hand-me-down jeans. When dad was born, Uncle Jack couldn't pronounce the name Richard, so he simply called my dad Sritch. That's a name that stuck for life.

Wearing nothing more than denim overalls, Sritch, Jack, and their friend Jimmy were barefooted, dirty, and free. That was the life for three boys who would fish when they wanted and sneak an occasional smoke when it was available. All those activities fell under the watchful eyes of parents who wielded the hammer of Thor when it came to discipline.

There was also extravagant love. One year, grandpa learned of a financially devastated family that would have no Christmas celebration or gifts. So, they packed a meal and extra presents and shared the holiday with those friends in need. It was the best Christmas dad could recall.

Dad remembered a boyhood that was more idyllic than oppressive—but the years tangled together to bring a wince of regret when it came to the eroding of dad's relationship with his parents. In his post-high school years, tensions mounted. One day dad had his fill and decided to show his parents once and for all who was boss. Without their prior knowledge, dad stealthily delivered what was sure to be the dominant move over his parents' firm hand; he joined the army. That would show them who the boss was.

But as the Kansas-bound bus pulled away from the station and dad looked back on his sobbing mother, his decision didn't feel all that satisfying. Quite the opposite; his heart broke along with grandma's. And, wouldn't you know it, the Army proved to be no retreat from the thumb of discipline and rules.

Military life was a lonely place for dad, no more so than when he found himself serving a tour in Iceland. The oppressive cold, the unrelenting darkness, and the bleak emptiness around him only made the divide between dad's heart and home seem all the wider. At least he had the visceral satisfaction of being on the crew that tended the Honest John rockets. On an arctic night, as the Northern Lights softly painted the skies, Richard Fish stood tall, honorably guarding the starkest symbols of the Cold War tensions.

I would love to have seen that slender, handsome young man in full uniform standing proudly in a field of Honest Johns with their baleful nuclear payloads.

In my hand today, I hold the aging medals for good conduct. Good conduct. That sounds like my father: a good soldier, a good man.

The escape plan from the discipline of home perhaps led to the discipline dad needed to set him on the path to strength and honor. But the harshness that dad wanted to avoid stayed with him, and at times, he would carry a heavy hand of discipline.

I remember my retreat to college seeming like the exit plan I needed from dad's strenuous, and sometimes harsh, measures of control and authority. Dad could be prone to flashes of anger, a trait I share.

Despite the fragility of the human skin that my dad and I have worn, there was always a more potent, mightier bond of love and uncompromising faithfulness. Though we walk the path of soil-bound men, we don't have to lock into behavior that hurts or damages others. That's the route that goodness takes. We try to do better with each generation, learn from past errors, and live more uprightly. Sometimes we succeed, and sometimes we don't.

The Bible tells us that even Paul had to reckon with an angry spirit and a harsh hand. Moses was no stranger to the overreach of an inner tempest. And Peter, who walked with and learned from the grace-filled presence of Jesus himself, still went with his impulse to wield a sword when his ire was drawn. Is there grace and mercy for those who wrestle with hard things while desiring to live a good and decent life? I have to think so. It's a gift of understanding that my dad left with me. It clings to the cluttered walls of my mind and reminds me that I can walk tall despite mistakes. I can be a good man without ever bearing the scrutiny and weight of greatness.

I know this to be true because I'm Richard's son.

5

– A Stranded Motorist and The Voice in the Darkness –

Those heavy army boots dad wore once crunched their way over Iceland's cold, brittle, U.S. rocket-lined military grounds. But when those lonely, dark days of service gave way to lonely, dark days rediscovering civilian life, dad had to find his voice in this world. Finding our voice involves learning to listen to other voices speaking into our lives.

Home had changed. Dad had changed. Those long stretches of road knitted through Bartholomew County in Southern Indiana seemed to lead nowhere.

Then one night, dad heard a new voice.

———

To say that my dad's brother Jack was also a legendary figure in my mind would not be an overstatement. My sister and I still consider that being like Uncle Jack is the gold standard for learning how to love each other's children. It was only as an adult that I finally knew how this man who called my dad Sritch was more significant to my life than I had ever imagined.

Around the time that we had to say goodbye to Uncle Jack and lay him to rest, dad unveiled something revelatory about their brotherly relationship.

"Jack was more than a brother to me," dad told me. "He was a spiritual father."

While dad was in the army, Uncle Jack had begun his family. He'd also laid out spiritual shoots that grew to deep, deep roots in an exciting church on the corner of 22nd and Maple in Columbus, Indiana. As the '60s unfolded, that little Free Methodist Church began to bloom and blossom. Many young families were finding common ground and spiritual refinement.

"Sritch, you need to git on in here and check out this church."

I can only imagine how Uncle Jack drew dad into the idea of experiencing life through the eyes of faith. It was an invitation that would profoundly affect generations to come. The invitation resulted in dad deciding to follow after and love Jesus with all of his heart, soul, mind, and strength.

———————

There was a long stretch of highway between the church and home. But it was a stretch of road that no longer seemed lonely and endless for dad. There was a new hope in his life, a new joy, a new peace unlike anything dad had ever experienced before.

But there came the night when, as dad traveled home from a church gathering, he would encounter what people today might refer to as a paradigm shift. Some folks call it an attitude adjustment. Something was about to happen that shaped how dad listened to God, completely changing how he looked at the world around him. It was the birth of a man that would live for others. A man willing to do good and right things.

The songs and scripture from that night's church gathering were still dancing in dad's heart when he noticed the stranded motorist with blinking hazard lights. Dad could see the car from a distance. And the closer he got to the car, the louder the voice in his head became.

"Richard, stop and help them. You need to stop. I want you to stop. You need to do this for me."

This brand-new voice was easy to shake off at first. But dad didn't want to stop. And so he didn't. But, the further he got from the driver needing assistance, the louder the voice.

"Go back. Help them. Go do it." The voice was adamant.

Dad would eventually learn to recognize the voice of God when it came. The Spirit would often prompt dad to help, to assist, to go to the side of someone in need.

That night, he could wrestle no more with the voice. He swiftly circled around and returned to the site.

It was a woman and her young son. As he took off with his two new passengers in tow, he heard words from the woman he would never forget, and they were words that became etched into his bones.

Seeing the Bible on dad's dashboard, she reached up, tapped the book, and said to her son, "You see. I told you if we prayed, God would send somebody."

I told you if we prayed, God would send somebody.

Some words remain on infinite repeat in our memory's storehouse.

Knowing how many people dad gave a helping hand to over the years, this story has historical significance. It always brings a tear of joy to my eyes. I almost feel like it's the origin story of a superhero. But it would have to be one of those superheroes with no superpowers, one a lot like you and me. A sense of goodness, mercy, and duty to help others would be the driving force.

Extraordinary lives are lived mainly by ordinary people. Greatness may be ascribed to some, but goodness stands in the breach and makes a difference.

Hearing the voice of God may not be as elusive as we think. Once we decide to follow after Jesus, we listen to the call to help others in need more clearly. Some will fault dad's generation for being too focused on being good and not enough in doing good. But I witnessed, first-hand, a man who discovered that BELIEVING means BEING. To believe is never sufficient. When grace does its work in us, it gives us an overflowing resource from which to draw. Grace can't stop with us; it cries out for us to provide it to others.

I've discovered such a peaceful contentment about taking up the good things that present themselves. As I pay attention, I might even recognize that God speaks to me in the call to serve, just like He called dad all those years ago.

I often need to be reminded to listen, keep my eyes open, and help when needed. It's a lesson I learned long ago because I'm Richard's son.

BECAUSE I'M RICHARD'S SON

6

- Bluegill -

There's a ripe and ready time of the morning when the sunlight has barely breached the horizon, and the blue gill are hungry and searching for a meal.

If you hit just the right farm pond at just the right moment while the summer day is still cool and fresh, you might be in for the fish fight of your life. You'll wrestle your poles and bug spray into a tiny john boat and push out into the water. Or, perhaps, you'll settle into an innertube with rubber flippers on your feet for navigating. Either way, the goal is intentionally positioning yourself to cast towards cattails or stick-ups. Once you place the bee moth on the hook of your Keystone jig and gently fling it towards the bank, be careful not to get it tangled around a log salmon.

Grandpa introduced me to that term. When his fishing line would get caught on a branch, he would exclaim, "I've caught a log salmon!"

Casting bluegill bait takes a certain finesse. It's lightweight and easy to overcast. Or undercast. It's embarrassing when the line whirrrrrs pathetically as the lure plops into the water a mere two feet in front of you. But as your fishing muscles awaken, the pole and line become extensions of your being, and it is as if you can will the bait to the perfect spot.

Within the first few casts of your line, you begin to connect with whatever lies below the surface. It's not unusual for the baby Bluegill to clean the bee moth off your jig. Sometimes, the babies will take full hold of the hook and come out of the water crying for their mother. You can only remove them from the snare and return them to the murky water with a quick flick of your wrist.

Soon, if a keeper is lurking and hungry, you're in for one of the great thrills of your day. When a pan-ready blue gill takes the bait, and you've properly set the hook, you will think you have a ten-pound whopper on the line. The bluegill is a fighter. He may not be the largest of the freshwater fish, but he puts up a big-boy struggle.

"Bring him in, son, bring him in!" Dad would laugh as he cheered me on in the battle between fishes. It was a competition to see if the water-dwelling variety had enough moxie to elude the man who bore the last name Fish.

"That one's a keeper, son," dad would proclaim. "I can clean that one just fine!"

And he could. Dad was a fish-cleaning virtuoso. Whether the catch of the day was sparse or bountiful, dad would whiz through one fish after the other with lightning speed. He would lay the fish out, skin it, filet it, then flip aside the remains in what surely must have been record time.

Bluegill was our favorite fish to eat. Bass was wonderful. Crappies were just fine. Even the occasional catfish was a joy to sizzle up in the pan. But to our humble estimation, none were better than our favorite member of the sunfish family, the beautiful bream. Bluegill.

Some of the best memories of my life are of dad and me wetting a line on peaceful waters. The two of us didn't always get along back in my growing-up years. I was different. I would rather play my guitar than work on a car with him. I was lousy at catching a baseball and had no interest in hunting.

But there was fishing. I loved it, and those fishing trips with dad are among the gold in the treasure chest of my mind.

From time to time, those sweet memories of my father return. When the day is ripe and ready, and the conditions are good, when the waters are still, and the line goes deep, my heart will latch on to another story of bygone days. As I reel it into my mind, somewhere in the distance, dad still cheers me on. "That one's a keeper, son! Bring it in."

Dad has been gone for too many years now. I say gone, but I know right where he is. He's still encouraging me from the banks of Heaven if such a divine observation is allowed. Dad is in my heart, occasionally in my actions, and always in my character.

I love the keepers. They sustain me; they feed my soul. Those beautiful memories serve as navigation points for my journey through life. Today, once again, I paddle my boat into position and artfully fling the line of my pole into the cattails of time. I anxiously wait for the next recollection to take hold, then I relish what I recall. And I never take those memories for granted. They help me to understand the ancient words from the Bible a bit better,

"Lead me by your truth and teach me,
for you are the God who saves me."
(Psalm 25:5, NLT)

We are all taught by the collection of ideologies that we learn to be true. Some will relate to my stories of dad, and some will find them to be foreign and strange. But each of us has learned from our own stories and encounters with life. My journey with dad taught me to understand that God's words are true, and I can learn from them and find my sense of direction.

I don't need a fishing pole in my hand to remember how to cast bluegill bait. It's muscle memory. Give me a pole and a pond, and I can find my target. I can finesse my way to the prize.

I learned how to do this because I've learned of the trustworthiness of my Father in heaven. I learned this because of the dependability of my earthly father; I know there is hope because I'm Richard's son.

7
– The Name I Hated –

I hated my last name.

How could there be a crueler last name than Fish to attach to anyone? It has been the source of endless jokes over the years. And yes, I've heard them all—every single solitary, fishy joke.

You should see the looks my family gets when it's time to be seated at our favorite seafood restaurant and the voice on the intercom beckons, "Fish, party of four. Fish. Your table is ready."

When people quizzically ask me to spell my last name, believing there had to be more to it than just F-I-S-H, I assure them that it's the same spelling as the creatures that swim. I throw in hand motions as a bonus, flattening my fingers and twitching them like a fish darting through the water.

I once had a fish tank, but it became too much maintenance for my preferences. I still collect unusual fish items. I have fish-shaped candy dishes and a walking cane with a fish-like handle. If it's unique, I might buy it. The walls of my home are decorated with clever wooden fish and paintings of finned creatures.

That's a pretty high level of embracing a name for someone who once disdained the very sound of it.

I wish I had the sense of humor about it as a child that I have now. If only I could have laughed at myself when kids would mock me rather than letting it hurt me to the core of my being and giving the jokesters the thrill of seeing me embarrassed. But then, that's simply not the nature of a child.

In my growing up years, there was a business in Indianapolis named L. Fish Furniture. They regularly advertised on the local television stations. The commercials often featured people in scuba gear dancing around a sofa and singing, "Fish for furniture!" Oh, how I hated that commercial.

One day as I boarded the bus that would take me to Mt. Healthy Elementary School, the kids at the rear of the bus began singing. I say singing, but in reality, it was a mix of taunting and singing.

"Fish fa fuhnicha, Fish fa fuhnicha."

One of my options would have been to make fun of how they couldn't correctly pronounce furniture. But that would have gotten me beaten up.

I know now that the perfect response would have been to cheerfully sing along with them and invite the other kids to do the same. I should have made it my anthem.

But instead, I hung my head low and tried to choke back tears. I quickly sat down near the front, sure that I was the most loathsome creature ever placed on earth. And the kids at the back of the bus just loved that.

One night as dad and I were in his truck, I broke the silence by telling him that I hated my name.

"Why did I have to be named Fish? It's the worst name ever! I hate that stupid name," I whined.

Dad spoke majestically into the moment. His admonition was so powerful and sacred that I believe it was directed word for word by God's Holy Spirit.

"Why son," dad said in an instructive yet assuring tone. "That's your grandpa's name. You're not ashamed of your grandpa, are you?"

No! No, I was not! I could never be ashamed of Grandpa Fish. He was a giant among men in my mind, a hero that I lionized. To my young mind, there was no way that he could ever have a single fault or flaw.

"No way! I love Grandpa Fish," I replied in full defensive mode.

"Well, son, that name is your grandpa's name," dad confidently explained. "And if your grandpa can carry that name, you can wear it with pride too."

I had never considered that, but at once, I knew that dad was correct. He had spoken wisdom of biblical proportion.

It would be swell if I could tell you that it immediately resolved any embarrassment I felt about being named Fish. It did not. But, it was the start of me embracing my name. Dad's words impacted me so profoundly I can still clearly hear his voice all these decades later.

With time, I realized that some of us are born with an automatic nickname. When your last name is Fish, no other nick is needed. However, that still doesn't stop some from adding bonus phrases. Fish Face. Fish Lips. Fishy Wishy. They've long since lost their cleverness, but I smile nonetheless and encourage them on. I often join their mocking tones with my own fishisms. And then… I make fun of their name. Is that wrong?

Children can often intuitively sense, then exploit, someone's weakest spots. We would never do that as adults, would we? Surely not.

I've come to understand that God can make even our weak spots strong. He has this way of holding us together so that weak and strong mesh into this glorious average. They come together in a sort of goodness. His strong right arm holds us up when we fall. Out of the ashes of failure and loss rises new hope and wonder, all to the voice of a Father who knows us well.

Perhaps we should once again unpack that prayer from earlier:

"Father, SHOW ME the way...

LEAD ME, and I will follow...

REMEMBER your unfailing love...

FORGET my failure...

My hope is in you."

Once we firmly establish our identity in the hope of our Father, God, we can find our way through the catcalls and harsh tones of earthly voices. It's all because we know who we are and where we belong. Our hope is in the Name that represents love, forgiveness, and mercy.

I can wear my name with pride because it came from a grandpa, and a father, who stands tall in my mind. I also proudly wear the name of a Father in Heaven who puts meaning and purpose into my broken days. I'm so glad I learned that lesson as a child. When greatness alludes me, hope finds me.

I wear my name well because I'm Richard's son.

STEPHANIE JOINED OUR FAMILY PICTURE.

I WAS MUCH HAPPIER TO WELCOME MY NEW SISTER THAN I APPEAR TO BE HERE.

8

– Sunday Mornings –

There was a cinnamon and Old Spice fragrance to the Sunday mornings of my growing-up years.

The kitchen belonged to dad on Sunday mornings, and breakfast would always be hot off the stove or out of the oven. On the best Sundays, we would be greeted by the smell of maple and brown sugar filling that sacred space. And always, in the hours before donning a dress shirt and tie, dad was there in his white t-shirt, freshly annointed with Old Spice after shave. His Sunday School book full of blue Bic pen marks would be splayed open on the kitchen table. All the while, he was stirring a pan or checking the oven.

Every page of my memory includes dad teaching Sunday School. There were young adult classes, teen classes, post-college, adult couples, and seniors. I remember the absolute devotion dad gave to instructing well. He took his studies seriously and prepared with the wise heart of a teacher. My sister, Stephanie, and I sat in dad's class before anyone else attended the formal gathering that would come later that Sunday morning. With typical Richard Fish excitement, he would share his thoughts on the day's topic. Thanks to that consistent example he lived before us, we learned how to lead.

We saw what it meant to do careful, prayerful preparation.

Let's return to Sunday breakfast for a moment. A coffee cake or some other cinnamon-infused baked good might await us on the best days. On the not-so-favorite weeks, there might be Cream of Wheat or a concoction we knew as Hot Ralston. It was a less-than-thrilling combination of grains that sat heavily in a child's mouth as they would try to swallow the mushy lump of cooked cereal. If fortune prevailed, a few drops of maple flavoring were added to ease the pain of ingesting what seemed then to be the equivalent of sawdust. In the midst of all of it was dad, the Sabbath breakfast chef, reliably preparing sweet delicacies or bidding us eat and stop complaining.

The drive to church included a reliable ritual, though it stands among the more unpleasant things I recall. Sunday morning would be the occasion when dad ruled the radio, and on that one day, playing the music loud was permissible. I use the word music generously. It's hard to describe the horrible screeches and belches that came out of the speakers as music. Like so many in that day, Dad was a big fan of the local Gospel music radio show, a nauseating miasma of local acts and so-called Christian comedians.

I used to complain that the singers weren't singing. They were bellowing. And the comedians? I recall that they had nothing funny to say but typically made the audience laugh by injecting strange noises into their patter. "An' then I went on in t' church, eeeee aaaaa! (*laughter*) My goodness, there was Miss Pansy in her green and pink moo moo, iiiiiii aaaaaa oooo eeee! (*laughter*)"

Something amusing would reliably happen on that radio show, and I got in trouble for laughing at it every time. The local announcer, who later became a friend of mine, had a very country-boy way with his pronunciation. Therefore the Traveling

Ambassadors became "The Travelin' Bastards." Though I hated the singing, I always looked forward to their appearance on the show, even if I had to learn to chuckle to myself. Oh, who am I kidding? I loved provoking dad just a little with my obnoxious snickers. It was never an offense punishable by a spanking, and I could handle the ice-cold, stink-eye glare I would get in the rearview mirror.

Dad was a big fan of the boxy passenger van of the 70s. He had many different rationalizations for why the van was essential to life. It would serve as a kinda-sorta sheltered pick-up truck. If you removed the back benches, which in days of old was a much bigger task than stowing today's fold-into-the-floor minivan seating, you could then pile the van full of several ricks of chopped firewood. A rick of wood was similar to a cord. I understood neither of those measurements, but dad seemed to instinctively be able to tell at a glance when he achieved a rick. There was also an art to stacking the wood properly to accomplish a tight, stable stack. It was an art form I never mastered as a young man, much to my dad's eternal frustration.

The other glorious purpose for the window-encircled monstrosity of a motor vehicle was that it served as dad's personal bus line. And for years, dad would ferry families and young, wayward men to church. And the one I recall affectionately was a man named Eugene.

I was sure that Eugene lived in a haunted house; that's what the massive Victorian structure resembled in my mind. Eugene had a room on the upper level. Dad would pull up, and, to my embarrassment, he would honk that freight-train-like, dead-man-waking horn. If the neighbors weren't awake yet, they were after dad arrived. Typically, we had to wait on Eugene. Sometimes he would stick his head out the window, rubbing his eyes or running his fingers through his bedhead hair, and either tell dad to stay or to go on without him. And then we'd wait longer. And longer.

When Eugene finally made it to the van, he introduced aromas to my life that were strange and curious to me. Looking back, I suspect it was akin to bacon meets barroom with hints of tobacco and a bit too much body odor. Even still, I took to him immediately. There was something affable and endearing in the way he loved our family. He was always asking questions and seemed to drink in any response. Whether he had questions about something he'd read in the Bible or inquiries about my week at school, he seemed genuinely engaged with whatever the answer might be that week.

Eventually, Eugene moved to another city for a good job. I heard that he drifted back into old lifestyles, and while I wasn't sure what that meant, I knew it wasn't good. My heart broke for my Sunday morning friend, though I can't help but think that dad's influence stayed with him in some vital way.

Dad had a rare passion for people. He had an evangelist's calling. He was active in the ministry for Jesus in ways that formed how I view the world. Some people talk a good game about helping people in need. Dad did it. Though he would always preach the gospel of hard work and clean living, his heart bent toward those who were in need, broken, and even addicted. In his last years, dad always had someone who became a project to him. There was always someone to lavish with love, care, and concern. Someone always needed a father figure, a little help, a break in life. Even at the risk of occasionally being taken advantage of, dad would be there for them.

It's amazing how helping someone who has lost their way helps you to find your way. As we allow God to bless others through our actions and generosity of resources, we, in turn, are blessed. I wonder if that's part of what the psalmist had in mind when he wrote,

"The Lord is good and does what is right;
he shows the proper path to those who go astray.
He leads the humble in doing right,
teaching them his way."
(Psalm 25:8-9, NLT)

There is a debate about what it looks like to follow Jesus. Does it impact our actions? Is there any transformation that moves us towards doing right things? What are right things, anyway?

Dad taught me that there is a right way, and that's what the psalmist is implying. On our own, we lose our sense of direction and end up in the weeds. But when we follow Jesus, we go down a path of doing what is good and right. While those actions don't save us, we learn their value because we are made new. So, as we humble ourselves and allow God to help us find our way, it's natural that He takes us down the path of doing good things for others in need. That's the way of the Father.

I discovered how good and right paths genuinely make a difference and how they truly serve to bless me in return because I'm Richard's son.

9

- Hands -

Visceral, deeply carved memories of dad live inside me like a pile of Moses' memorial stones. I bump into them every day.

I remember dad's strong, firm embrace. It was like hugging a sandbag; solid, yet just right. Dad's arms were the personification of the Biblical reminder of the strong arm of God lifting us. I understand more about God's fortifying power because I saw it on display in my dad.

Holding dad's hand had a unique way of reassuring me that I was in the watch of a capable, caring man. His hands were rugged and calloused; I could feel every ridge and crease as he gripped my hand firmly. I knew that I was holding the paw of a hard-working man and never had any doubt that he was working hard, in part, for me.

Familiar fragrances often trigger our strongest memories. I often think about breathing in the full of dad from all the years in his presence. Sometimes it was the fragrance of an Old Spice man. Sometimes it was the earthiness of an outdoorsman. Sometimes, late in the evening, it was the putrid stench of well-traveled feet being relieved from their shoes and filling the room with their funk. All these things remind me that dad was, faults and humanity and all, more than just a legendary figure in my past. He was real. He was human. And it was good to walk with him through life.

Though dad was a rough-edged, strenuous country boy, he was also an artist. The same hands that magically melded with wrenches and rakes could also find comfort in colored chalk. Later in life, his artistic flair turned to woodworking. He was not your classical artist, but Richard Fish had a folk art flair that was a powerful expression of his character.

Dad had perfected something that he called a chalk talk. He would teach life lessons while bringing an image to life, sometimes working with blacklight. He relished starting with one drawing and surprising the viewer when it turned into something unexpected. The lessons he taught reflected his conservative theological view. There was little room for ambiguity when he taught about the dangers of sin and then specifically named the sins he had in mind.

Around the age of 12, I developed an interest in puppetry. Dad quickly encouraged me by writing a chalk talk routine involving dialogue with my puppet. He would construct no usual puppet screen for me to hide behind as I lofted a puppet high into the air. Nope. Dad invented a puppet screen that allowed me to sit directly behind the puppet, hidden by a curtain, while I rested my elbow on a table. This technique helped me to maintain the stamina to hold the puppet up for an extended time while he chalk-talked. Only now do I properly appreciate dad's clever problem-solving abilities.

Dad's hands were the hands of an inventor. Convinced that he could solve the mystery of perpetual motion, he worked to create a magnet-driven machine that would operate under its own power. He left that idea on the drawing board.

From heating our home to storing fishing rods, dad had no limit to his ideas. And as for his son, I also float on an endless flow of dreams. Mine are less mechanical, but there is no doubt as to why I'm gifted with the trait of boundlessly developing ideas.

————————

Dad was a wood stove man. Our home's primary heat source was the iron-hot, old-fashioned wood-burning stove ensconced upon a stone-tiled platform dad had laid. Every winter, our ranch-style home boasted a roasting hot family room at one end and ice-cold bedrooms at the other. But there was something nice about how that blazing fire could warm you all the way to your soul.

The wood stove created a constant demand for wood; gathering wood was a job my dad found exhilarating. He loved firing up that ear-splitting chain saw, bringing down trees, and piecing them into logs. My job was to split and pile. He loved to joke that I was his pilot. He would cut it, and I would pile it.

Naturally, dad could slice through a piece of wood with an ax like a table knife through butter. On the other hand, I struggled to divide the imposing log properly.

"Son, you gotta grunt when you swing the ax. Then, let the ax do the work," he insisted.

He would yell, "HOOEY!" as he gracefully arched the ax overhead into the fibers of the wood, creating two pieces where there was one.

It was a puzzle to me how to let the ax do all the work AND add the grunts and hollers to make me stronger. Those two ideas didn't fit together, yet they made perfect sense in dad-logic. He was correct.

I gingerly lifted the menacing axehead high into the air, behind my back, and around again to the front. I bellowed an exaggerated "HOOEY!" mocking how dad would say such a silly word. But dad would laugh when the log split perfectly down the center as my axe met with the wood's fiber. "See, son, I told ya. I told ya."

I am a man who was formed, in part, by the roughest, toughest hands. I was formed, in part, by hands full of love and artistry. I was formed, in part, by hands that could resuscitate a piece of machinery, and yet I come to this point in my life with no mechanical skills. I was formed, in part, by hands that were more reassuring than any GPS when it came to giving guidance, even though there were times when that guidance fell upon my backside.

"Son, did you pick these green tomatoes?" Dad asked while kneeling to get eye-to-eye with four-year-old me.

It is one of my earliest memories of learning my lesson about gardening. Those green tomatoes seemed irresistible as my young hand effortlessly plucked them from the vine and dropped them to the ground. It turns out my tomato-picking venture was unwise, and I had to learn to respect the growing process.

"I don't want to do this, son, but I'm going to have to spank you."

Looking back, those spankings never really hurt my bottom. But they jarred something loose inside of me that I needed to confront. The pain wasn't the whooping. It was the pain of learning, the pain of growing. It was a moment that demanded that I stop, pay attention, and decide what to do with my error. To be clear, I'm not advocating raising a hand to a child. But there was a deliberate gentleness often present in the discipline of those days that was important to its era and probably better left there. Can you tell that I struggle with this issue?

The hands of a man who struggled against the wood and the weeds of this world guided me. I was built by hands that both lifted in praise to God and lifted heavy tools to split wood.

Wouldn't it be nice if we could physically see the hand of God pointing us in the right direction at times? OK, so maybe that would be a bit jarring to see. Nevertheless, we often find ourselves pleading with God for an answer. "Where should I go now?" "What should I do next?"

God gave us strong hands to deal with creation. We work it, shape it, and make it suitable for living. But when God created it all, He simply spoke. So while His hands may not physically point the way, His words do.

As surely as God moved me with His words, I've been moved by the strong hand of an earthly father.

I've known the power of rugged hands because I'm Richard's son.

RICHARD'S SON

10

- The Finger -

Dad spent most of his years working as a machine repairman at Cummins Engine Company. He liked to joke that Cummins could go into the shoe business because they already had 10,000 loafers.

There was a cast of characters that dad worked with, men with unusual names that stirred cartoonish images in my mind. I heard of the workplace adventures of Gravy Gut, Hop-along, No Comb, and John Wayne.

Gravy Gut would bring an entire cooked chicken for lunch each day. I'll leave it to your imagination to ponder how he got his nickname.

Hop-along had a bad leg. Therefore, according to dad's stories, he would hop along.

No Comb? Not a hair on his head.

And John Wayne? Well, that was his name. You need no nickname when you're born with a moniker like John Wayne.

I often wondered if these were real people or just stories that dad had concocted. But to a young man, there is nothing cooler than hearing stories about guys named Gravy Gut and Hop-along.

"Tell me that one about No Comb again, dad!"

"Well, you see, we filled his work locker up with combs, and he chased ol' Buckeye around the plant for an hour."

"Buckeye? Who was Buckeye?"

"Well, that rascal has a locker right next to Booger Face...."

———

There was a problem with one of the manufacturing machines that dad needed to repair, and he instructed the operator to shut it off.

"I need to clean this out," he explained.

After getting the all-clear, he reached back inside the machine with his rag.

CLANK.

Down came a machine arm, severing dad's right index finger in two. Dad would later have a less than flattering assessment of the machine operator's intellectual capacity for understanding the meaning of the words "Shut it off."

At this point, many of us may have passed out. Or, we might have grabbed our hand while loudly expressing our displeasure at what just happened. We may have waited for a medic to arrive to care for our divided digit. But if you think Richard Fish did any of these things, you clearly have never met the man.

What happened next seems like family folklore. It was recounted so matter-of-factly by dad that we never doubted its veracity.

Dad reached over, calmly grabbed the part of his finger that had been so ungraciously removed, and began walking toward the nurse's station. He figured he must've been in shock, but no one around him could tell. On the way, a guard asked, "Hey, Fish, what are you up to?"

"Oh, I just got my finger cut off," dad replied in the most unflustered way possible.

Assuming dad was joking… I mean, come on, who picks up their finger and serenely walks to the medical area?… the guard pulled his pocket open and said, "Just put your finger in here."

Dad said that if he'd been in his right mind, he would have done just that. Instead, dad held up his bleeding hand, and the guard turned white as a mid-winter snowfall.

When you lose an appendage working at a big company plant, you get paid a compensatory amount. That was the case when dad experienced his amateur amputation. They had dollar figures attached for every contingency, figuring out how many knuckle joints were lost and what body parts were affected. There were better ways to profit from this plan than losing a finger. I've often wondered if the largest jackpot would be to lose your head.

Not only did dad enjoy a minor windfall for his misfortune, but it provided him with one of his favorite jokes to tell for the remainder of his life. He would be known to tell a kid that his nose has teeth, and it bit his finger off as he tried to pick it. Actually, that's pretty funny.

It seems that while I was hearing stories about dad's oddly

nicknamed co-workers, they were also hearing stories about me. But there was no joke attached, only pride. They knew of my achievements, my dreams, and my talents. Even though I enjoyed different things than dad, he was still proud of me. Imagine that. I found this out at his funeral.

As I stood there with the family greeting the guests who came to pay their last respects, a man with a pronounced limp walked up to me. "They used t'call me Hop-along," he said. I listened to his words with reverential awe. There truly was a Hop-along!

"Your daddy made a difference in my life. He's the reason I finally became a Christian. I was havin' a real hard time, an' your daddy came over to my house. He invited me to say yes to Jesus, an' I done it."

Then there was the squinty-eyed, Popeye-looking, bald guy. "I'm No Comb," the man explained in hushed tones. "Your daddy was a fine man. That man lived what he believed."

Later, a man ambled up and said, "Howdy, Pilgrim, I'm John Wayne." OK, so he didn't introduce himself that way, but it would have been so cool if he had. "You don't know me, but my name's John Wayne… like the actor."

"I do know you! I do know you!" echoed excitedly in the quiet of my mind.

"Your daddy was one of a kind. A real friend. Buddy, he was the real deal."

Dad's faith in Jesus was always on prominent display to his co-workers. He had a reputation, alright, and it was the reputation of being the man you go to when you truly felt lost.

Over the years I'd often hear dad express regret that he never did well in school. But by the day of his retirement, I'm convinced he had the equivalent of a master's degree education. After years of training and experience, dad had a keen intellect and insight into the mechanical workings of Cummins Engine Company.

So much of my life has been shaped by my father's impeccable reputation. I immediately had the respect of others simply because I was his son. Even today, some of the highest praise I receive comes when I'm compared to my dad in some way. I always feel honored to be a part of his legacy, even though I rarely feel I've earned it. And when life has wounded me, I do my best to calmly proceed forward, perhaps making a joke at my own expense but walking as tall and brave as I can.

I've learned the value of character and integrity because I'm Richard's son.

11

- The Vacation -

Vacationing under the leadership of Richard Fish was always an adventure.

Dad's mission was to ensure my sister and I could say we had been in as many of the 48 contiguous states as possible. And Canada. That didn't necessarily mean taking in the wealth of beauty each state holds; it simply meant driving through them on whatever interstate or highway could best serve the cause. As a result, dad would often go miles out of the way just to add another star to the flag of states we'd traveled, even if we had barely seen the area.

One other vacationing technique that dad routinely employed was staying on the go. Non-stop. We would wake up early and hit the road. Whether the day held a tourist destination or hours on the road, there was no lolly-gagging or dilly-dallying around. No sir.

In 1976, the bicentennial year, it made sense to take the family to Washington, D.C. But containing a vacation to just the nation's capital was not something dad could orchestrate. The trip had to be grander; it would be our chance to visit the region, and we were going to see it all. First, it was Niagara Falls, with a ceremoniously brief drive in and out of Canada. Then on to Foggy Bottoms for a spectacular whizzing through the Smithsonian, national monuments, and the capital building. Does that sound like a complete vacation? If so, you haven't paid adequate attention, my friend.

Before heading home to Indiana, we swung through West Virginia, where dad had heard about a steam engine train that would locomote up the side of a mountain, and we were going to ride that bad boy.

I'm not belittling dad's ability to engineer a vacation. I still treasure the memories of every trip we took, even if they were getaways that would have made Speedy Gonzalez proud. But that constant movement left us all frazzled with each other. That, and one other factor I shall now mention.

Taking in so many touristy locales can be taxing on the ol' budget. Dad's solution tended to be a combination of the cheapest motels possible and occasional camping. In the van.

Yes, you heard me correctly. We were a family of four, sleeping in a van. Not the minivan of the soccer mom variety. This vehicle was the big boxy van of the 1970s. Oh, and it was not the pimped-out RV-style vans you sometimes see. Dad removed the back bench to create a storage/sleeping area for him and mom, and a removable platform was placed over the front seats for us kids. It was a platform that, including the mattress, elevated us to nose-against-the-top-of-the-van height. And brother, was it ever sweaty hot sleeping up there. Why, it was enough to make tensions fly from even the mildest-natured child, which is a descriptor I'm certain applied to me.

It was by the campfire in West Virginia that I finally came unglued. I don't recall what I did, but it was an offense punishable by the old-school whooping.

Let me stop here and wrestle with the concept of spanking for one more inglorious moment. I have mixed feelings about the practice of corporal punishment. When I was a child, I was very much against it. Today we tangle with the topic with necessary seriousness considering the prevalence of abuse towards children. Spankings were very common in eras past. I'll let you surmise what you will on the topic, only to say that my dad's hard hands were also hands of great love and generosity.

Let's go back to the campfire now.

Dad took me firmly by the arm and led me to a secluded, wooded area. It was a short journey that felt like a hundred miles. I was a dead man walking. The lump in my throat felt enormous, but the knot in my stomach was even bigger. I knew that I had fallen out of favor for a moment, and I was about to feel dad's wrath delivered firmly on my hind regions. My mind raced. Could I reason with him? No, too late for that. Dad was always very committed to all decisions of a punitive nature. Should I run for it? No, I was 11. I couldn't survive out there. Should I get on my knees and beg for mercy? That sounds like a reasonable approach now that I think about it. But the solution that nestled into my brain was much more bizarre and unexpected. Once we arrived at the point of execution, dad glared at me and said, "Son, you know what is about to happen, don't you?"

Why yes, yes I did. With surgical precision and quickness that even impresses me today, I was able to unfasten my belt all at once and remove it with the speed of Barry Allen. I began to flagellate myself with the fervor of a political stump speech. I whipped my back, I whipped my butt, I whipped my legs, all the while proclaiming my guilt and shame. "I deserve this; I did it. I deserve this."

I remember the look on dad's face. It was a look of total shock, absolute bewilderment, and perhaps even a tinge of remorse. I don't know how long my pitiful attempt to avoid dad's belt went on, but I'm convinced it was much longer and much more ferocious than any lashing he was about to apply.

When I finished, as the tears ran down my cheeks, I heard dad say, "Well, I guess you got the point."

Was that it? Had I avoided the corrective hands of my father? Yes, I had; but it seems I entered the hurricane trying to avoid a breeze. My wrath against myself was far greater than anything I might have otherwise received.

As we returned to the campsite, there was no compassion at my mother's side. "Well," she asked dad firmly, "Did you spank him?"

"No," he responded. "He spanked himself."

Without missing a beat, mom shot back, "That's the dumbest thing I've ever heard."

When it comes to meting out justice for my failures and follies, I suspect I'm much harder on myself than our God of grace and mercy could ever be. I imagine that I am the vilest offender when I know I've broken God's heart. Perhaps this time, I've failed Him beyond his capacity to forgive. I wallow in contempt for myself. As if still thrashing the belt around in that Appalachian campgrounds, I deliver blows of self-loathing that God could never condone. It wasn't his intent to condemn me, after all. He went to the cross to overcome death and bear the sins of the world. He took the nails, wore the stripes, and bled until there was no more blood to give. The simple cure is confession and repentance. It's the age-old teaching that still remedies the brokenness of guilt.

I see now that dad never really wanted to punish me. No matter how angry he might have ever been at me, there is no blow that could have made him feel good.

In dad's later years, he apologized to me for being harsh at times. As dad and I stood there, it was as if he was now removing his belt to deliver blows of guilt and shame on his own backside. But I couldn't have that. I quickly told him that all was well because all was well. I thanked him for loving me enough to guide me, even if it might have been too hard for me to bear at the time. How else am I to understand those days?

After all, dad's punishment never became abuse, even in its most severe. Those moments of pain were so incredibly few in the light of all the beautiful ways dad's great love and compassion for my sister and I was on display.

Those break-neck vacations were dad's big-hearted gifts of love to us, and they are gifts I will treasure as long as I draw breath. On those family vacations, we found our way through state after state, site after site. And in moments of disobedience, I found my way to clearer thinking via my father's stern words and firm hand. As those days echo through my heart and soul, I recognize God directed me down many different roads for my learning and pleasure. I'm convinced that just as God is a wise educator, he must also have the heartiest laugh. It makes me smile to wonder if God was there by that West Virginia camp sight, face-palming in bewildered amusement at this character He created when He gave breath to me.

I have learned much about traveling the roads of life because I'm Richard's son.

UNCLE SANTA CLAUSE.
DAD & MOM WITH UNCLE JACK.
I THINK THIS MAY HAVE BEEN TAKEN AT
CHRISTMAS TIME.

12

– The Rabbit –

You can get 50 to 60 miles per gallon on cheap diesel fuel. At least, that was the way it was told to dad. And he was sold.

As the 1970s gave way to the '80s, the harsh economic realities ushered in a new trend. And it's a trend that would significantly impact my family.

The Nixon/Carter era was a glorious time for a bulky, roomy mode of transportation simply known as the van. And as the years of that decade passed, the van became more gaudy and blinged out. Dad seriously considered buying one of those fake wood and shag carpet-encrusted wonders. Considering that all passengers had those glorious captain's chairs to ride in, the van seemed like the zenith of comfort and style. It was the luxurious way to travel and camp; the cramped space led to innovations like pop tops and fold-down chairs that became beds.

Alas, dad would stick to the big, boxy, window-laden wonders that eventually gave way to the paired-down mini-van trend. But then dad heard about the Rabbit.

Being a machine repairman for Cummins Engine Company,

dad was already well-versed in diesel engines. But in the era where gasoline prices began to skyrocket and scarcity became an issue, the diesel car seemed to be music to the billfold of many weary travelers. Fueled by the claims of friends that their new little Volkswagen Rabbits were getting nearly 60 miles per gallon, dad was sold. Later he would discover that mileage in the upper 40s was the best he could achieve.

The small economy car movement had reached the garage of the Fish household, and it would change how we rolled into the Reagan era.

For the first time, my dad was about to purchase a brand-new car, fresh off the showroom floor, still smelling of newly minted vinyl and plastic. The pilgrimage to the Louisville, Kentucky showroom of the region's preeminent VW dealer netted our family a dark green Rabbit, the vehicle then thought to be the heir apparent to the Beatle.

The little four-on-the-floor stick-shifting egg beater was so precisely engineered for economy that it even had a yellow arrow that would light up and tell you the exact moment to shift up. Follow the light, and save money and fuel.

I would call that car our space shuttle. Just as NASA's finest would scrunch into a tiny compartment to be fired into space, rattling and shaking, we hunkered into the namesake of a small, furry mammal and rattled on down the road. At high enough speeds, you could feel every bump on the road.

But this little metal mobile was more than just a simple conveyance for the Fish family. Oh, my friend, it was so much more.

Too much more.

We experienced vacations in the Rabbit. A family of four, with luggage stuffed into an overhead carrier precariously strapped to the car top. There was minimal legroom and even less separation from the person who occasionally seemed to be my arch-enemy, my sister,

Stephanie.

"Dad, she's on my side!"

"Mom, his stuff is touching me!"

Riding together in the back of the space shuttle turned out to be a fate equal to being chained in a dungeon.

With the wisdom time has granted me, I'm sure that the drag from the luggage carrier on top of the car probably did away with any mileage advantage achieved by driving that minuscule machine.

Though I never became friendly with the stick shift, that verdant little VW would be the car I learned to drive in. It would shuttle the family to church each Sunday morning, except on days so cold that the diesel would gel and any plan to worship would come grinding to a halt on a country roadside.

At first, the novelty of owning a new car caused mom and dad to do something I had never seen them do before. And it only lasted for a short time. They cleaned out the garage to properly protect their prized investment.

My parents were probably low-grade hoarders, and it's a proclivity I've had to fight against in my life. For most of our lives, our garage was nearly impassible, stacked from top to bottom with boxes of treasures. Or junk. Probably mostly junk. There were boxes of collectibles that tended to be collectible in name only. There were old vinyl albums that might have some value today had they been appropriately stored, and household items that had worn out their welcome inside but still merited a spot in our storage jungle.

But in the first winter of 1980, my parents managed to clean a spot for our new Volkswagen Rabbit. I'm not sure what they did with all the junk it displaced, but I know that soon, new clutter would replace the VW, and the car found a spot on the gravel driveway of our home there in the rural expanses of southern Indiana.

By the mid-80s, I was entrenched in life at Greenville College, a small Illinois institution about a four-hour drive from home. The day came when I received a phone call about a passing in the family. Not a death, mind you, but the VW Rabbit had been passed on to a new owner in lieu of a pre-owned Oldsmobile. I had thought there was great affection for the rattling rodent VW in my mother's heart, but she was relieved to say goodbye. It turns out she was only supporting dad's desire for an economical ride, and she found the gut-shaking Rabbit to be as undesirable a mode of transportation as I had. As mom proudly told me of her comfortable new dusty-blue Olds, I realized an era had ended.

"I just don't understand why we're not getting better gas mileage," dad would say as he carefully wrote down and calculated the numbers. Every gallon of fuel added to the Rabbit and every mile drove was recorded in that little spiral-bound glove-compartment notebook. At the end of every line was a number that furrowed into my dad's brow; 46, 48, 44, 47, 48, 49. But never 50.

"Just do what those other people do, dad, and lie," I said, convinced of my comedic genius.

A scowl would come my way as dad glared. It was the kind of heated glare that would have come with red fire beams attached had dad been Kryptonian. Even minus the fire beams, I was scorched into submissive silence.

I've been in the place where my best ideas and dreams didn't pan out the way I wanted. I have enough of my dad in me to beat myself up over failures to achieve the things my friends seemed to accomplish easily. Some days the numbers don't add up. Sometimes the family would get upset at my folly.

What do we do with days when best intentions get away from

us like a rabbit racing for its hole? No matter how great someone else might think we are, those moments of personal revelation remind us we are frail mortals. It's those delicate moments where the strong right arm of a mighty God sure is a welcome relief. Our plans can get frustrated and brittle, but God has a much larger view.

No matter how disastrously wrecked our best-laid plans become, there is a gentle peace in finding that we still haven't lost our sense of direction. When God is directing our path, we can maintain our bearings. "The Lord is good and does what is right; he shows the proper path to those who go astray." (Psalm 25:8, NLT)

I've seen a good man buoyed by the grace and renewal of God.

I was in the back seat watching it all because I'm Richard's son.

13

– Two Wheels and a Ditch –

Richard Fish was a biker. Sort of. Over his last decades, he became a dedicated bicyclist, becoming increasingly knowledgeable about the science behind bicycles.

However, he might have become a motorcycle biker had it not been for one fortuitously located backyard bump at our rural home outside Columbus, Indiana.

There was this silver-ish Honda that buzzed like one of dad's chainsaws. It seemed to barely be a motorcycle, perhaps more a motor, seat, and handles connected by some feint sort of two-wheeled magic. It was small, it was unimpressive, and it was dad's.

It only took one ride behind dad to convince me that this was not the conveyance upon which I preferred to experience life. Every rock and pit and crevice on the road became a jolt to the senses when encountered by dad's bike. I clung to him for dear life, mostly with eyes closed, not at all sharing his adventuresome spirit when it came to this buzzing, fume-spewing contraption.

There came the moment in time when dad thought it would be fun to ride the bike in circles around our house. While our four acres nestled among trees and farmland in southern Indiana seemed spacious, it could barely contain the enthusiasm dad felt for testing the limits of his machine.

That bump I mentioned in our yard appears at this point in the story. In my mind, I see dad floating through the air as the bike spun towards the house, and his body did the roll-and-spin maneuver towards the sprawling garden he so lovingly cultivated.

Perhaps it was a miracle, or maybe it is easily explainable through dumb-luck physics, but neither dad nor the Honda was harmed in the mishap. At least, that was the case, so far as my sister and I could tell.

Since mom wasn't present, we received strict instructions that there was no need for her to find out about this little misadventure. But somehow, she found out. It was information too good to keep sealed in our souls.

Mysteriously, the motorcycle would disappear in the coming days, never to be spoken of again until I write these words.

Later, dad would take up a love for bicycles, which opened the door for its share of marital friction. Dad's desire to take off for long adventure rides on his bike was a bit more than mom could bear, and it wasn't until mom's passing and dad's marriage to Sharon that he found the cycling partner that tolerated his need for two-wheeled, self-powered speed and excitement.

That excitement would, at least on one occasion, result in a significantly broken bone. But the adventurous spirit never subsided.

As the standard bicycle became increasingly difficult for dad to ride comfortably, he invested in a recumbent bike, which allows you to stay in a natural seated position, low to the ground, and look like the circus is coming to town to any onlooker.

For winter riding, dad bought a large, brown spandex wrap that would go around the bike to shield the rider from the weather. "It looks like the Oscar Meyer Weiner-mo-bike," I sarcastically posited. That was a perfectly witty and accurate observation, but it was met with the stern, silent, stink-eyed glare I could often evoke from dad.

My favorite recollections of dad do not involve his passion for two-wheels. But, they do remind me of dad's strength, his off-center way of approaching life, and his ability to move forward through life despite the obstacles. His strong, stubborn independence was always tethered powerfully to a strong, stubborn commitment to family, friends, and serving God. I may not share his adventurous spirit, but I certainly have grown as a man through his lessons of commitment, character, and determination.

Our bumps and rough spots in life define us for better or worse. It is in those moments that we are made. In those moments, we decide whether to learn something and grow or fade into the murky gloom. I wonder if that's what the psalmist had in mind when he said God teaches the humble to do right. To find our way begins with a teachable spirit.

I've learned a lot about what it means to be a man of character because I'm Richard's son.

BECAUSE I'M RICHARD'S SON

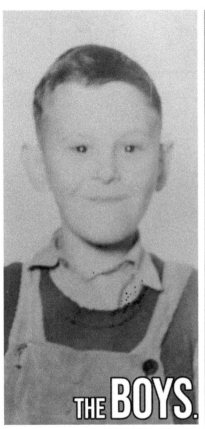

THE BOYS.
DAD AND ME, TAKEN A FEW YEARS APART.

14

- As Easy As Riding a Bike -

I learned how to ride a bike in the days before hyper-vigilance prevailed. I learned to ride with no helmet, no knee pads, and no elbow pads. I learned to ride on a full-sized adult bike. I learned to ride on a bumpy, serrated gravel road.

Can anyone tell how this story is going to end?

Thanks to a childhood injury, my sense of balance and coordination has always been off. I was a late bloomer to the joys of bike riding. Though I had a child-sized bike with training wheels, I could never master it. My inability to glide astride my two-wheeled nemesis led me to cast it aside into the old, leaky barn and walk away from any hope of ever learning to ride.

But Richard Fish was not the type of man who would allow his child to give up and withdraw from any challenge. It simply was not in our DNA. Correction: it was not in dad's DNA. I was willing to walk away.

The old, purple, single-speed bicycle was sitting in the yard, taunting me as it stood kick-stand upright.

"Gregory!"

Dad was calling. Everything I never wanted to do began with my proper first name. If mom called for such purposes, my middle name was added.

"Gregory! Come here, son. Today, you learn how to ride a bike," dad solemnly proclaimed.

Now, I mentioned that our road was gravel. More accurately, it was an engineered chip-and-seal road. All the fun and danger of rocks, held together by a cement epoxy, allowing it never to give way.

And did I mention I was wearing shorts? No knee pads? I just thought you should know.

As the bumps and jagged edges of the road jarred my ever-loving soul into an unsettled state of fear, dad ran along beside me, holding the back of the bike seat.

There's a seductive feel to how the wind fallows your hair as two wheels gain speed. Riding a bike is a rite of passage that allows mastery of time and space at the youngest of ages. I could feel the hesitations shed away as I fell in sync with that metal contraption. And then...

I glanced to my side and realized dad was no longer there. He had let go, and I was flying solo.

My hands quivered, and the front wheel began to convulse from side to side. Every rock on that road bounced me epically like a ship on a stormy sea. Confidence eroded, and just as quickly, my sense of balance alluded me. As I tilted to the side, my knee was unceremoniously introduced to the snagging and snarling chip-and-seal road.

"Son, what happened? You were doing it!" Dad asked and asserted as he ran to my rescue.

I didn't see it that way. I was angry, bleeding, and my pride was broken.

"Why did you let me go?!?! I'll never do this again!!!" I proclaimed through the tears.

Spoiler alert: I did it again. And again. And again.

I became quite masterful at the art of bike riding, even though I still bear the scar that reminds me of that first fateful journey.

The school bus stopped in front of our yellow-brick ranch-style home in the rural reaches outside Columbus, Indiana.

"Wow, look at that! Check that out!"

The kids in the bus were clambering about the shiny blue bicycle that stood kick-stand upright next to a smiling man. As I debarked, I was puzzled. It wasn't my birthday. It was just a regular old day. But that beautiful five-speed bicycle stood waiting for me to ride it through the hills and hollers of my life. And for a moment, I was the envy of every kid on the bus—even the bullies.

I was speechless as dad proudly proclaimed me king and owner of this regal Schwinn. And I was so lost for the proper response that I gave none.

Later, mom came stomping back to my room.

"Gregory Scott, I'm ashamed of you. Your dad was so excited to give you that bicycle, and you never said thank you," she scolded.

I understand that mom was ashamed of my response, not her son. But at that moment, I was also heartbroken and embarrassed by my misdeeds. I felt so sick to my stomach that I could have puked. One of my life gifts from God is this weird ability to empathize deeply with the emotions of others. That day, I felt disappointment deep in my marrow.

With tears in my eyes, I apologized and said thanks in the same clumsy sentence.

"Oh, son, that's OK," dad reassured me. "I just want you to know how proud I am of you for taking on this challenge. You did it, son. You did it."

If there were a way to call dad up today, I would do it to say thank you one more time.

I haven't always relished taking on the leviathans of life, but as surely as I call Richard Fish my father, there is a measure of godly strength that rises inside of me when I face something that seems too big to overcome.

Even standing beside a hospital bed the day my wife took her hand from mine, grabbed hold of her waiting Savior, and slipped away from my reach, I felt a strength inside born of this man who taught me how to ride a bike. As much as I wish dad could have been with me when my wife, Barbara, died, I am confident he was with me in spirit. I again took a breath, lifted my eyes towards the heavens, and found Richard-Fish-bred determination to keep moving forward even though I'd fallen.

I hope to share the strength of a good man with you. You have a Father in Heaven that cheers you on even as he lets go of the bike so you can learn to ride. He showers us with good blessings that we may or may not deserve so that we know we can do life well. We can dare to do good things.

I have learned a balance of heart that nature could not give me. I learned it because I'm Richard's son.

15

– And Now, a Recipe for Homemade Ice Cream –

Everyone else had those fancy schmancy electric homemade ice cream makers. We had the dumb old crank one.

I assessed it to be dumb primarily because of all the work it takes to operate a manual ice cream maker to produce the finest dessert ever contrived, equaled only by my mom's highly vaunted persimmon pudding.

Dad must have been one of those homemade ice cream purists. A renaissance man of sorts. Just as he was ahead of his time with his love of organic gardening, he would fit in today with those who think vinyl records and hand-cranked ice cream machines are the only things a person of quality and character should invite into their carbon imprint.

Here's how we made homemade ice cream.

Mom would prepare the homemade ice cream juice. This was no highfalutin crème anglaise my friend. Nope. This sweet nectar of the regular folks was the beginning of the best vanilla ice cream a person could eat. It included strange potions known as Milnot and evaporated milk.

Over the years, I have sampled many homemade ice creams seeking to dethrone my mom's version in the desert pantheon of my mind. Frankly, I have tasted better ice creams. But mom's version is sacred and divine and forever awarded my gold medal—no need for discussion.

Outside that yellow brick ranch-style house, my dad would be hard at work in front of the opened garage door. For anything to be good, it simply could not be easy. Or at least, that served Richard-Fish-logic well. So, not only would the best homemade ice cream require a hand-cranked oaken bucket, but even the ice had to be a labor of love. Dad would go to the freezer and pull out old milk cartons that served as giant ice cube trays. He would peel away the cardboard carton and bust the cube into small segments with a hammer. There would be no ready-made, bagged, cubed ice for dad.

But now, for the devious part. I'd speculate that this next phase is almost sinister and would have made fence-paintin' Tom Sawyer proud.

Dad convinced my sister and me that cranking that old ice cream maker was more fun than any human should be allowed, and we would battle over who got to crank first. One would crank, and one would sit on the machine to hold it down. The whole contraption worked like this: place the beater inside the canister, secure the canister in the center, load in ice chunks and copious amounts of salt, and place old newspapers over the top to insulate. The newspaper would serve to separate the hiney of the child, sitting on top thinking they were participating in one of life's most glorious moments, from the chunky, frosty ice. All the while, the other child cranks away until their arm separates at the elbow.

The final step of the ice cream-making process was for the brother and sister to become exhausted, leaving dad to crank through the last, most laborious turns.

And then, there was ice cream. Refreshing homemade ice cream. We were the richest people on the face of the earth in those glorious days when the hand-cranked ice cream machine came out.

What happened to that old crank-style ice cream freezer? It's probably now owned by some hipster listening to awful hipster music on vinyl.

Now that I consider it, it's kinda sorta crazy how hard work could produce such divine, heaven-touching moments in life. I wonder if this was some sort of Richard Fish conspiracy to teach me to love working hard and to be grateful for the results.

Or, maybe, it was just a way to make a delicious dessert.

Either way, I am richer and not afraid of crank handles or sitting on top of a bucket of ice. I experience life at its best and goodest because I'm Richard's son.

16

– The Greatest Fish
Story Ever Told –

I finally fell asleep, tucked under the makeshift lean-to consisting of a blue tarp and foraged tree branches. The magnificent night sky speckled with stardust watched over our sleep as the age-old pines stood guard duty in the surrounding hillside.

That lean-to was enough to keep the dew off of Dad and me as we snuck in an hour or two of sleep between rounds of fishing throughout the night.

My sleep was interrupted by an unexpected sensation. It felt as though something had fallen on my face. I'm not sure who was more startled as I suddenly sat up - the bullfrog that had decided my face was as good a landing spot as any or me. The old croaker hopped off into the water as I did my best Three-Stooges-style-face-smacking, trying to wipe away any yucky stuff the frog left behind.

"Son, what's a'matter with you?" dad asked groggily as the commotion awakened him.

"A bullfrog just landed on my face," I muttered as I blew out some spit for good measure.

"Go back to sleep," he growled, rolling over on his side.

"Go back to sleep. Ugh. A frog just landed on my face. Ugh. Yuck. Pteww…"

Somewhere deep in Hoosier National Forest lies a glorious body of water that only dad seemed to know. "Dad, are we safe fishing there?" I would inquire.

"Why do you think I'm bringing my pistol?" he would reply.

Dad was a lot like Jesus. Questions were often answered with another question.

We loaded up, strapped on backpacks, inner tubes, and coolers, then headed out for the one-mile trek through the woods. We would finally reach the lake, where we would unload our gear and prepare the ritual of moving it all to a small island. I would take the inner tube across first, and then we would ferry the night's supplies over with a rope attached to the other tube. Finally, dad would make his way across. Occasionally a friend or cousin would join us.

We knew a special secret about that lake. While I established early on that dad and I preferred to catch bluegill, the real prize when you were fishing these secluded waters was the catfish. Off and on throughout the night, they would begin biting on chicken livers, and we would catch what dad called a mess of fish.

The fishing was great, but the communion with dad there on that tiny, peaceful island was the most special thing.

There was always way more lunch meat, eggs, bacon, and Tootsie pops than we could devour on one trip. But then, such a sublime occasion called for the proper feast, and dad knew how to do it up right.

Billy Gilbert joined us out there once. While dad and I had reasonably good fortune with the fish, poor Billy didn't catch a thing all night. His misery was exacerbated by the fact that his thermos of coffee had been left at home. All night we heard the sad song of a man who was sure the fish would accept his bait if only he had a cup of coffee. By morning we thought he had finally bemoaned his plight for the last time. But sitting out there on the brown water, fog rising with the dawn, Billy looked around and sadly intoned, "Ohhhh my... this lake looks like one giant cup of coffee. I wish I had me some coffee. I'm just sure I could catch some fish if I only had my coffee." We laughed, and we fished.

There was another occasion when one of dad's cousins came along. That, my friends, is the night that I caught 14 fish at the same time. On ONE line. And that is no fish story, either.

The chicken livers were working. The catfish were biting as the damp early morning hours began to wrap around us. And they were beauties—one after another. We were slaying them.

Dad didn't trust the basket his cousin was using to keep the fish in. The heavy catfish went into this wire basket, then back into the water to keep them alive. But, the basket was affixed to the bank by a tiny stob. "Oh, they'll be just fine," we were assured.

After catching catfish number 15, dad's cousin began feeling around on the bank for the stob and chain. It was gone.

"Boys, I hate to tell you this. But you were right. I lost the fish," he confessed.

We were sick about the mishap, but the waters were lively. One after another, we continued to lay into the generously proportioned cats. And then it happened.

It was the tug of all tugs. My pole swayed over until I thought it would surely break. And the line was moving. That much resistance usually would mean that I was caught on a branch. But this action had a lot more life to it. Had I just caught the king of all catfish? Had I just hooked a trophy-worthy lunker? Dad's face lit up, but it wasn't at the thought of the size of one single fish.

"I wonder... I wonder if we're about to experience something special here," dad said with all the gusto of a schoolboy.

Slowly, slowly, slowly, I began the arduous process of reeling in my catch. "Be careful, son, be careful," dad reminded me. He could have taken my pole and brought it in himself, but he let the moment be all mine.

As the line shortened, dad got on his stomach and reached down into the water. With a whoop that only my dad could muster, he gloriously pulled the wire basket from the water. It was the basket containing our original catch. It had somehow floated right into my line, and that night, I landed 14 fish at the same time on ONE line. I hope the Guinness folks are paying attention because it's undoubtedly a world record that has never been bested.

Those nights in Hoosier National Forrest have faded into memories now. The deep bellows of the face-landing bullfrog and the steam off the early morning brown water resembling an exquisite cup of coffee have all danced away into the expansive sky. Nights catching catfish have been replaced by days wistfully remembering those treasured experiences with dad.

Life has taken me far and away from those incredible fetes of fishing. Though there have been many other lakes and many other peaceful nights spent smacking mosquitos to the sound of happily lapping waters, there have been none like those long-past golden encounters on inner tubes and beneath lean-tos, with a bright fire warming our spirits as the fish willingly accepted our offerings.

I can't help but wonder if there will be fishing in Heaven. I'm OK with the thought that there will be. I believe there will be lakes, islands, campfires, and fishing poles in the sweet by and by. I imagine dear Billy Gilbert will be gleefully sipping from a cup of coffee while landing one fish after another.

Perhaps that's overly imaginative thinking. Or perhaps that's just the longing of the heart of a weary traveler who will one day be home with a Heavenly Father who loves to give good gifts to His children. I won't stop counting the blessings he gives me while I'm still earthbound. But I'm also eagerly longing to know just what divine encounters await on the banks of the rivers of eternity. It keeps me fishing. It keeps me faithful. It keeps me ready to tell the story of 14 fish caught at once while wondering what greater catches await.

God seems to have a particular affinity for fish. He used one to move Jonah from one place to the next. Jesus surrounded himself with fishermen. He multiplied fish to feed hungry crowds and knew of a fish with a coin in his mouth when funds were running low. He willed massive numbers of fish into nets when fishing was terrible, and he fried up an inviting pan full of seafood for breakfast when his followers were dispirited and dejected. Don't tell me there won't be fishing on the new Earth that God is preparing. He's highly invested in the water-bound segment of His creation. I can almost smell those celestial fish fries now.

It may seem strange to imagine Heaven like that, but there could be no other way for me to envision the hope of what is yet to come. It's quite natural, after all, because I'm Richard's son.

17

- Sacred Spaces -

There's a peculiar little fruit that I've come to discover is native to my home state, and it's called the persimmon.

You'll find persimmons outside Indiana, but I've rarely encountered anyone outside the Hoosier state familiar with this magical little quarter-sized piece of heaven. It's a berry, but nothing like the berries you might imagine.

Persimmons are harvested in the fall. Most of the trees simply grow in the wild, which meant that finding persimmons was an adventure that required great strategy. Once the fruit is ripe, you must gather them quickly because deer also have a taste for this natural treasure.

While there are different varieties of persimmon around the world, Indiana persimmons are much smaller, with a deep autumnal orange hue. Their flavor is unique, though I once heard someone describe them as similar to a fig. You can serve persimmon in various ways, including cookies, fudge, ice cream, and cakes. My preference is a delectable dish that stands out as one of my all-time favorites: the persimmon pudding. And my mother's was the best. Trust me.

When I say pudding, you might immediately think of chocolate, butterscotch, or tapioca pudding. But it's nothing like that. Persimmon pudding, when made correctly, is a moist, dense cake. Mom would top it off with a sweet, thick caramel-like glaze.

There's one more thing you should know about procuring persimmons. You should only gather the ones that have fallen to the ground. Ripe persimmons fall from the tree.

As a young boy, I was convinced that dad was forcing us to bend over and pick up the fallen persimmons simply to create extra work for us. After all, the teeming branches were low enough that I could have reached up and harvested the fruit without stooping or crouching.

"Dad, why can't we pick all these off the tree?" I asked with layers of frustration in my voice.

There came the day when dad decided to teach me an important life lesson, and it was a lesson I shall never forget.

"Well, son, why don't you just go ahead and pick one and eat it," he devilishly obliged.

I was determined to show up dad as I triumphantly plucked the orangish berry from the branch, removed the stiff leaves from the stem, and plunked the fruit into my mouth. School was now in session. You see, an unripe persimmon is one of the most bracingly bitter things you can ever put into your mouth. Far worse than any lemon you may have ever bitten, these little fruits create an instant pucker that has come to sit a spell when it visits your face.

I spat. I puckered. I groaned. Dad laughed. Lesson learned.

While we don't know for sure what the fruit was that Adam and Eve ate in the Garden of Eden, history has supposed that it was an apple. I say otherwise. I believe that Adam and Eve plucked a persimmon from the tree, bit it, and we've all been puckering ever since.

In years past, I might have told you that Christmas was the best time of the year. But looking back, the autumns of my boyhood were chock full of rich, fragrant memories that still send waves of joy through my soul. If heaven allows such a thing, I might request to go back and have a wiener roast at the edge of the woods behind the house where I grew up. Those events are sacred in my mind. Those were moments when dad created a genuinely enthralling happening for all who would come.

There could never be enough wiener roasts in the fall. Sometimes we'd invite family: other times, folks from the church. And on occasion, it could even be just dad and me. Those were spectacular hours.

Dad and I would gather branches for a small bonfire, carve the end of a green sapling clean, and poke it through the finest sausage concoction of all, my beloved red dog. A red dog is probably, in essence, pure junk. But it is divine junk. Sometimes we'd call them fat dogs for their larger-than-usual shape. But they would always be held in a red casing that would pop, crack, and split open as we roasted them over the fire. Once delivered to the bun, the only suitable toppings were yellow mustard and relish. As you bite into a fire-roasted red dog, grease rolls down the side of your face, and ten hours is automatically deducted from the span of your life for eating such garbage. And it is worth every bite.

As much as I loved red dogs cooked over an open fire, being alone in that sacred space with dad was the highlight. No fizzy bottle of pop or bag of chips could ever accompany a moment like that as nicely as simply sharing space with dad.

"Want another dog, son?"

"No, dad, let's just sit here for a while."

"Sounds good to me."

———⌐———

When friends or family would join us for wiener roasts, there would be rituals that were as predictable as any family Thanksgiving tradition.

There would be the sweet aroma of persimmon pudding wafting through the house. Dad would be outside dragging logs into place for seating, then building and stoking a magnificent bonfire.

As darkness began to frost the October landscape, cars would arrive. Doors would slam shut, and happy voices could be heard from the distance. The closer you get to the wooded area where the greatest of events is about to unfold, your feet begin crunching over more and more fragrant, fallen leaves. The smell of burning wood greeted your nose, and that hot orange glow would warm your face.

It was important to select a thin but strong sapling branch and carve the end to needle-like precision. The correct way to skewer the hotdog was in a parallel fashion, end-to-end, though that required a certain exactitude so that you didn't merely split the dog in two. Some would demonstrate inexperience by threading the hot dog onto the stick from the middle in the shape of a T. That was a recipe for disaster. Those neophytes often ended up losing their meaty morsel to the fire.

After marshmallows had been roasted and faces and fingers were sticky and white, it would be time to gather around the fire for stories. And the highlight of the night would be dad's recounting of Tailey-Po.

We'd never get enough of the tale of the old man who lived in the woods by himself and how one day, he chopped off a tail sticking out from a log from some creature hiding underneath. He took the tail back to his cabin and made soup. But late in the night, a voice came crying out from deep in the woods.

Dad would slowly pace around the fire, hunched over with arms extended wide. In hushed, spooky tones, he'd say, "That ol' voice kep' on a-sayin', 'You know and I know all I want's my tailey-po. You know and I know all I want's my tailey-po.'"

Softly, slowly, methodically, he'd weave the tale while looking for the one who, not having heard the story before, was utterly spellbound by the legend. Suddenly, dad would jump toward the poor, unsuspecting victim and shout, "You got my tailey-po!" Screams would ensue. If we were lucky, someone would fall off their log in fear. The rest of the guests would roar with laughter. No matter how often I heard dad tell that story, the payoff was always worth the wait.

The spot where we held those wiener roasts was a place where heaven touched earth. It was a sacred space. Sometimes, I'd explore that precious spot and look up to the sky when alone. There, I'd see a perfect circle burnt into the canopy of trees from years of blazing fires. Or perhaps, it was a portal that God had placed there so that we could be transported into his presence every fall.

It is a true crime that our government never saw fit to declare that ground a sacred national monument. It's a shame because in the years after mom died and dad sold that house and property, some in-gracious lout built a garage and created a junkyard of cars over that space. It was a profanity of the highest degree. Did they not realize how precious that ground was? Could they not feel the power of the history emanating from that space?

Just as surely as dad is gone now, so is any chance that I'll be able to visit those days in my mortal body.

But just as certainly as dad walked there, and just as surely as he created an event that so electrifies my memories, that place and those days will never leave me.

For a moment each fall, dad was Walt Disney, creating a wonderland and weaving tales, and authoring adventures that no one there will ever forget. I am convinced that God uses sacred places and occasions like these to draw us closer, to hold us tight. There are times in the passing of our days when we might not sing church songs or utter a single scripture verse. But even still, Heaven closes in. The breath of God breathes heavily all around us, and we feel content, joyful, and at peace. In those perfect moments, life is a gift from Heaven, replete with God's unfailing love and abiding presence.

My memories are ablaze with the simplest stillness and the most perfect, smoke-infused happiness because I'm Richard's son.

18

– The Man Sitting Next To Me –

The picture of high-school-aged boys in filthy t-shirts and jeans, heads buried under the hood of a car with wrenches and greasy rags lying around, is as Americana as it gets. But, growing up, you would never find me hovering over an engine block.

Dad would never have admitted this, but I suspect there was probably at least a twinge of disappointment that I had no interest in cars. At least, not the gunk-under-the-fingernails, spark-plug-adjusting, oil-soaked interest that he had. OK, so it was even worse than that. I never really appreciated classic cars and could barely tell you the difference between American Motors and General Motors.

I don't believe dad was ever disappointed in me as his son, but I'm sure he would have loved for me to have at least a little gasoline in my blood.

Many times, dad tried to turn me on to all things mechanical. Anything relating to a moving vehicle was second nature to him. When a car had a problem, he'd call me to the driveway and explain how to fix the seemingly insurmountable issue. And it always went something like this:

1. Take the part out,

2. See what's wrong with it,

3. Fix it,

4. Put it back in.

To him, it was that simple. To me, it may as well have been a 50,000-piece puzzle of a solid color. Dad would eventually get frustrated by my lack of interest or understanding and send me on my way. I'd gladly go pick up my guitar and play. I understood the guitar. I could change guitar strings, tune it, and play it with the same ease that dad could carburate a carburetor or manhandle a manifold.

Dad's metric for buying a car was as simple as his process for fixing one. The vehicle should be American-made (or, in the case of the VW he once bought, made on our shores), low-mileage, and sturdily built. That last one was always up to dad's interpretation.

One of the first cars I ever test-drove as a newly licensed driver was a brownish-orangish-bluish-colored AMC Gremlin. It had originally been just a blue Gremlin, but now the flecks of remaining paint were precariously knitted together by vast expanses of rust. Those glass-bottom tourist boats in Florida had nothing on this little beast - I was treated to a thrilling view of the gravely country road beneath me as I took it for a spin. Maybe spin isn't the best choice of words. I pedaled that death trap and held on to the steering wheel for all I was worth. Upon returning to the owner's field, where it had been unceremoniously parked, dad and I looked at each other with wide-eyed headshakes. It was a unanimous no, one of those rare moments when dad and I saw eye to eye during those years.

———————————⌐————————————

"So what kind of car do you like?" dad queried.

I had just asked him what I should buy. I assumed he would know and be ready to tell me. I was unprepared for the decision to be wrested back onto my shoulders.

It's not that I had that high-paying dream job every young man fresh out of college wants. It was my first gig in radio, and I would have wrestled those microphones and turned the potentiometers for next to nothing. And next to nothing was precisely what I got paid. But with my naive young commitment to budgeting and saving, a modest new-to-me car was within reach.

"I can't tell you what do get, son. What do you like?"

I named a few models that came to mind. I wasn't sure how they looked. Or how they drove. Or where they were built. Or even if they were sturdy.

Dad was holding back a snicker. "Son, that's an old-man car."

Oh. OK. I may have seen it on The Price is Right. It was Bob Barker's fault that I selected an old-man car.

Eventually, the Chevy Celebrity met both the eye appeal and the budget test. Once I honed in on the perfect make and model, dad finally voiced his approval. The winning one was eggshell white.

There was never any question as to where I would go for financing. Dad took me to his "man at the bank," which is a bygone concept. What I wouldn't give to have an ongoing relationship of trust with one person at a bank. Today's corporately-owned banking has taken care of that once and for all. I certainly love my corporate bank app when it comes to all its deposit-online coolness. But I'd give it up for a man or woman at the bank.

So, picture this. We walked into the tiny office, and the man greeted my dad by name, and they shook hands. A few moments of small talk ensued. Then, my dad confidently says, "This is my son, Gregory." That's what I got called when I met the man at the bank. "This is my son, and I'd like you to give him a car loan."

What happened next defies all manner of logic and reason in today's banking culture. But right there in the Cummins Credit Union in 1987, my dad's man at the bank responded with, "Yes, sir!" He then pulled out a piece of paper to gather my information. Keep in mind the loan was already mine. He even offered me a bank credit card if I wanted. I got the credit card. Before paperwork, with no credit score scam to pound me down in my young years, I was offered and given a credit card.

I was an onlooker, in awe of a process that seemed so easy. It would never be that easy again. As I sat there, I knew that I was not getting that car loan because of anything I had done. I was getting that car loan because of the man sitting next to me. My blue-collar dad's reputation in the banking world of that day was unimpeachable.

Just like that lost moment at the loan officer's desk, so much of who I am and what I've gained in this world is because of that man sitting next to me. Purchasing my first car, understanding the beauty of helping others, working hard with a hoe and a shovel, and knowing how and why we walk with Jesus; it was the man sitting next to me that opened so many doors for me.

Part of praying to find our way, to gain a sense of direction in this life of twists and turns, involves asking God to remember His compassion and undying love. I'm pretty sure God doesn't forget; I'm equally sure we need a trigger to remind us that love is God's prime trait. It signifies great power and authority when you can love someone despite their abysmal failures. This mighty God is the one who sits with us in the loan offices of life. He's the one on whose authority we move through life. It's the blessing of His goodness that prevails.

Noone walks an easy road. But it's the man there with us that truly brings peace and stillness to our souls. He is the one that helps us find our way down the road when, otherwise, we would be abandoned to ourselves.

I don't move forward because of anything great I've manufactured on my own, just like I didn't get that loan because I am Greg Fish. I got it because I'm Richard's son.

19

- Iced Tea and Pie -

Richard Fish was a country boy through and through. It showed up in his dialect, it showed up in his musical tastes, and it showed up in his work ethic.

Today we minimize fathers by relegating them to man caves and belittling their attempts at humor by dismissing them as dad jokes. Interestingly, the jokes my dad once made were embarrassing to me when they fell from his lips repeatedly, but today I hold them in my heart as part of my treasure chest of memories.

I've always loved iced tea, and I'm a heavy drinker when it comes to that thirst-quenching beverage. My mother's iced tea was the best as far as I'm concerned, and I drank it like a thirsty man in the desert. If we had company for a meal, I reliably knew what was coming about the time I poured my third glassful from mom's reddish-pink glass pitcher that seems like a classic relic to me today. Dad would proudly tell our guests that I was like the ol' Indian that liked to drink iced tea. "Yep," he laughed, "Til one day they found that Indian dead in his tea pee." No matter how often he told that joke, he would laugh as if it were a freshly minted play on words.

I carefully conjecture that it was permissible for dad to make a joke like that since his grandmother was Cherokee. Regardless, it was never about Native Americans but always about me. And I felt put down by the joke that I heard what seemed like hundreds of times over my growing-up years. I failed to realize then that dad used humor to express love, just as I've done countless times over the years. If I can understand that principle when it comes to me, why couldn't I get it when it came to dad's jokes?

When I would come home from college between semesters, dad had an all-new joke to needle me with on infinite repeat. "I'm not too impressed with that college Greg is going to," he'd opine. "I asked him what he'd been learning, and he tells me, 'Pi R squared.' I can't believe I'm paying all that money for him to learn that. After all, everyone knows pie are round!"

The amount of satisfaction that dad got from that joke was equal to my humiliation. I have a different perspective on that today. Dad would readily admit that he barely made it through high school. And through his life, he bore the internal weight of feeling like his "book learning" didn't rise to an acceptable level. Never mind that dad likely had a Master's Degree worth of knowledge accumulated as a machine repairman at Cummins Engine Company. Not to mention the fine skills he'd mastered as an exemplary gardener. Truly, dad surpassed any measure I could place on him, and I wish I'd done a better job expressing that to him.

I found it easy to dismiss a father with such an unusual grasp of English. To him, the state of Hawaii was "Hi-wi-ya." A bow and arrow was a "bow-n-narry." And when he had to make a lot of turns on the road, he would say that the route "wee-wi's" around. Oh, how I'd love to hear those beautiful colloquialisms again.

I'm sure that I'm not the only one who has ever experienced embarrassment over a dad's sense of humor or use of language. But from the vantage point of having lived beyond the so-called middle ages, I look back with great fondness at these unique gifts that dotted my life with dad. My sister and I often recall these things with wistful smiles and perhaps even pangs of grief over what we've lost.

In the Old Testament, God once commanded his followers to construct memorials made up of stacked rocks so they would remember what God had done for them in that place. Today, memories like the ones I carry of my father are stacked rocks that remind me of how richly God has blessed me. Some stones may represent things that embarrassed me at the time, but now, they are a part of my life that is an honor to recall. It reminds me that God has always been present and that He has built something in me to remind me who I am and who He is making me.

I have that gift of recollection that lifts me with joy, hope, and peace because I'm Richard's son.

20

- Real Men Cry -

Someone that I loved once told me that real men don't cry. But I know they do.

While I may have gotten my ability to easily shed tears as an inheritance from my mother, there were a few times when I saw my dad cry. And one of those occasions hollowed out my soul.

In the days right after I graduated from high school in the summer of 1983, Grandpa Glenn Fish died. The final pictures of him show a ghostly white, unwell man.

He was a godly leader in his family and a nearly iconic, legendary figure in my memory. As the years pass, the pedestal I place grandpa on only rises higher.

Three ministers gathered to eulogize grandpa collectively. But it was the Right Reverend Broadwith, or Brother Dud as he was also known, that was to go down in infamy. Wide-eyed and dumbstruck, we listened as he spoke in doom-ridden tones worthy of any Vincent Price movie.

"Death is waiting around the corner to grab us up! Death looms, waiting to snatch us away from our loved ones. Death is a grimacing shadow monster, rising from the fog to grab us up!"

The day would be saved, though, by Brother Mel, who sweetly reminded us at the graveside that grandpa had now laid down his baton, and we had the privilege of picking it up and running on, holding it high. It was an image that would shape my life; I could see myself taking all the good things from this good man and letting them live on through the good things I could also do in this world.

It was at grandpa's funeral, amidst a nauseatingly sweet miasma of funeral flowers and candy peppermints, that I uttered one of the most asinine observations that could ever pass through the lips of a 17-year-old.

"Mom, dad's crying!" I foolishly whispered.

"Of course he is. That's his daddy," she rebelliously whispered back in wintergreen-infused tones of indignity.

There were ample free peppermint candies laying about just waiting to tame the breath of any funeral attendee, but we were a wintergreen Lifesaver family.

The sight of dad standing at the casket, wiping away tears, was a watershed moment for me. Shockwaves ran through me as this staunchly controlled man I knew as my Father was doing something I'd never seen him do before that moment. It made such an impression on me I blurted out that puerile statement.

It turns out that wouldn't be my last encounter with the tears of the man of steel. That was only an introduction to the tenderness and fragility of a man whose roughness and toughness had guided me through my formative years.

This is the second time I heard dad cry.

Mom and dad's 25th year of marriage had been a strange and wonderful journey. Mom had been sick off and on throughout 1989, and she was so proud that she was losing weight with so little effort. But there was also intense stomach pain.

In early summer, they had taken the trip of a lifetime to Hawaii. Before lifting off on that celebratory tropic vacation, dad revealed a surprise he had in store for mom. And it showed me a romantic side of my father that was nearly as surprising as his tears at grandpa's funeral.

"I want to make a tape for your mom with special songs and a special message. I'm going to play it for her on the airplane. I'm going to need a small tape player. And headphones for us both. Can you help me out with that, son?" he asked.

I smiled. "Sure, dad. I'd love to."

"Oh. I almost forgot. There's this song I've heard. 'You're in my heart, you're in my mind...' can you get that for me?"

I smiled at the sweetness. I smiled because my southern Gospel-centric dad knew a Rod Stewart song. I smiled because I knew, without a doubt, that mom would cry at 32,000 feet as dad played the tape for her inflight to Hawaii.

She did, of course.

So many threads came together to make my parent's 25th year of marriage a tour de force. They were constantly off on another trip or finding time for date nights. It seemed as if their marriage had never been stronger or grander. And then the threads began to unravel.

By midsummer, there were too many red flags. There were too many signs that something was going gravely awry in mom. 1989 was the year that the dastardly demon of cancer hissed its way into my seemingly untouchable family.

―――――――

The receptionist at the radio station where I worked found me in the studio to tell me my dad was on the line. I felt like I had a lump the size of Rhode Island in my throat. Rhode Island may be a small state, but it makes for a pretty large throat lump.

Dad called me from the surgeon's office, where the consultation had just taken place. How bad would this newly discovered cancer in my mother prove to be?

"Son, we're going to have to storm the gates of Heaven," he cried.

I could never forget those words; they are tattooed on my soul. It wasn't even the words, though I knew they spoke of dad's desperation. It wasn't uncommon for dad to call me to prayer over a difficult situation. But this time, the words came in wavering tones from an unwavering man, words soaked in tears and brokenness. And it broke me. I could barely bear the heaviness of the moment, the thickness of the despair.

―――――――

I love Wendy's hamburgers. I mean, they are thick, juicy, and fresh. Top that with a Frosty, and life is good. But dad's phone call earlier that day seemed to take all the enjoyment out of that dining experience. It was a good place to meet them to hide from the pain. Nobody wants to cry at Wendy's.

In those years, I lived at home. My first real job was in the next county over, and it allowed me to pay off my stifling college debt without high living expenses. But it also meant I could not run to a safe place to hide. The air at home was weaponized with a paralyzing new reality. I did not know how to talk to mom about this discovery. The conversation that had always been easy would now be fitted with new, more onerous words. I simply didn't want to talk about it at all. So here was my strategy: I had stopped to buy a bud vase for mom. Surely that single flower would express my heart without the need for tedious discussion.

I am that weird personality type that likes talking about my deep emotions. But that evening, I wasn't even in sync with myself.

I placed that flower on the kitchen table and scurried to my room where I planned to hide from reality. But there weren't enough covers on the bed to keep the moment from finding me.

"Greg, come here," mom called out.

My flower had been discovered. My desperate run to my room had given me away.

"Greg, come here." It wasn't a threat. It was my mother knowing my pain and calling me near.

There are places in this life that can become sacred. In the kitchen of that brick ranch-style home, right between the table and the stove, is a sacred spot. With no words said, my mother and I held each other and wept. There was an overwhelming, overabundant flow of tears and sobs.

Then it happened. It was something that galvanized that already unforgettable moment.

I didn't realize that dad was standing nearby. But as I hugged mom as tightly as I could, I unexpectedly felt his two muscular arms wrap around us. It was an anguished grip, the kind of hold you hope will keep your beloved from slipping away. But it wasn't just dad's embrace. It was his tears. Dad's guttural, fortissimo sobbing still reverberates in the hollers and backroads of my mind.

All we could do was cry.

It wouldn't be the last time I heard dad cry. But oh, how it changed my world. Could a man so strong become so weak?

Sometimes a good man has to walk on two roads at once. Goodness leads you to find a way to celebrate the joy and wonder of life even while you brush up next to a pain so awful it conspires to drag you straight to the doors of hell itself. I don't know what greatness does in a moment like that, but I know what goodness does.

I know that goodness embraces its loved ones in the tightest of holds and cries with them. It stands strong, firm, and secure on shaking legs. I might cry more than my dad ever did, but I also stand strong through those tears. The waves of death might pound against me. I might spend countless days in cold, gray hospital waiting rooms. Pain might be poured out at my doorstep. Betrayal might seize my breath. Still, I can breathe in the goodness of God's presence. It resuscitates me. It renews me. It's the blessing that comes out of the pain.

Real men do cry. How can that be understood in light of the fact that we are made in the image of God? Could it be that God is there embracing us and sobbing right along with us in our most significant moments of despair? Could his strong arms be wrapped around us, holding us together when we're about to fall apart?

There is no disgrace in tears. There is, however, a hope that we don't have to live in a place of sorrow. We can move forward, make progress, and take in a new breath of life. God, our Father, is near to the brokenhearted, and He holds all things together. That's one of the central promises I've clung to in my life. And it was exemplified to me in living color and full stereo sound that day in the kitchen of the home where I grew up.

I can feel the embrace of the Father because I'm Richard's son.

21

– And She Was Just 47 Years Old –

The words came out of me in a casual, unmeasured way. "I'm going to ask dad to be my best man."

I thought that would simply be a passing snippet of information no more important than a department store receipt. But they were words that brought glad-hearted tears to my mother's eyes.

Sadly, mom would not be able to attend the wedding.

As I survey my life, incredible losses have always accompanied tremendous gains. In the autumn of 1989, I lost my mother to cancer. It struck more swiftly and efficiently than any of us imagined it could. But in those days of letting go, I also took hold of a blessing that would shape my life for the better. Those were also the days when my relationship with dad grew deeper, stronger, and thicker. In those days, dad taught me, more than ever before, how to walk like a man.

"God, please let me stay with my kids. Let me see my grandchildren."

That was the prayer of the mortally wounded; it was the petition of a woman who needed just one spare crumb of hope. It was my mother's prayer.

That Wednesday evening, the altar of the Columbus, Indiana, Free Methodist church was full of friends who had come to support my mother in prayer. I remember mom kneeling at the altar, sobbing with a rare ferocity. I wrapped my arm around her, and dad's hands were on our backs.

Years later, my sister would tell of how her babies would sometimes look off into the distance with a smile and tiny laugh that could not be explained by anything she had done. It was the type of response a baby would make to, let's say, a grandmother's smiles and soft words. Could it be that mom's prayers to see her grandbabies got answered in a way we could never have imagined? I don't worry too much about whether that's good theology or not. I will find out with time. But I do know God has blessed us with the ability to imagine and wonder, which can be very reassuring.

I buried my head deep into my pillow as my mother cried in agony. One of dad's regular tasks that autumn was to clean and change her drainage system installed as part of her surgery. The sound of mom's tear-filled moans was sickening. Dad had to do this act out of love and necessity. I knew deep inside that I could never do such an onerous task, even for one I love.

Little did I know. Little did I know.

Years later, dad told me that he admired how I looked after my wife as her long-term illness presented me with responsibilities I never aspired to do. It's no wonder I could meet the need of the moment; I had a good teacher.

As mom zig-zagged between hospitals near and far, dad loyally attended to her with his presence, gifts, and prayers. There would be respites at home where we thought mom was surely on the road to full recovery and remission. Those days were illusions, and earthly healing was not to come.

In my younger years, Gene's Cafeteria was one of our town's better dining experiences. And on a day when dad, Stephanie, and I needed a comforting meal away from the hospital, it was the perfect retreat. But that was also the day I noticed it for the first time. Just as dad had been faithfully by mom's side, holding her up as best he could, my sister and I were doing the same for him. It's almost as if he was hobbled. His arms were around our shoulders, and we were helping him to walk. In those days, dad was a tired man struggling to stay upright. His breath had been taken from him, and his muscular frame had lost its power.

"I don't know what I'd do without you kids," he told us as we slowly comforted ourselves with food. "You two will have to help me walk for a while."

Of course, there was nothing wrong with his legs. It was his spirit that was flagging.

I remember feeling proud that I could walk with my dad through those grueling days. It was the first time I remember feeling the weight of being a man in a dying world. Even as I was lending strength to him, I was learning how to be strong, exercise extreme care for those I love, and rid myself of my own needs to give someone else just what they need at that moment.

Barbara and I began dating just a few weeks into mom's ordeal. Mom met Barbara for the first time in an Indianapolis hospital room as I brought my beautiful new girl for a visit. There was an instant affection between the two. But as Barbara and I grew closer, mom grew weaker and weaker.

After barely more than a month of dating, Barbara and I knew we wanted to spend the rest of our lives together. If we wanted mom to be at the wedding, we needed to act quickly. So we began planning a late-December wedding. And mom was thrilled.

There are some days in our lives that we can almost remember moment for moment. The Sunday before Thanksgiving of 1989 was that day for me.

There was a holiday meal at the church, followed by a special evening worship event held in what we called the chapel. It once was the church's main sanctuary and it contained many precious memories for those older than me. It was the room where dad's life was changed when his brother Jack invited him to attend. And it turns out that room would come to hold one of the most precious memories of my life.

That was also the evening when a young man I had grown up with came to an altar of prayer to find his way back to Jesus. I had never done anything like this before, but as God nudged me - actually, He tugged at every bone in my body - I found myself at my friend's side, praying with him in this historic moment. It was a time of spiritual maturing and bonding that shaped my life. It was also the night I would hold my mom for a thousand years.

After the service, I felt myself walking on the clouds of the present heaven. And there was my mother, looking at me with a "This is my son in whom I am well pleased" kind of gaze. As I saw her there, feeling the presence of all things heavenly, I got a glimpse of her in her earthly frailty. We met in the aisle of that chapel and began to hug. I felt strangely sure that this would be an important hug, and I'd better make it last. I remember it down to the very words that crossed my mind.

"I need to make this moment last for a thousand years."

To this day, I am still partly in that embrace with the woman who walked beside me for the first 24 years of my life. She is still with me.

The next day before I headed off to work, I stopped by mom's room. She always insisted that I tell her goodbye, even if it meant waking her. What a terrible headache she had that morning. Later, I would get the call that she had been taken to the hospital because of the excruciating pain. I took in a deep breath and thought, "Well, at least she's going back in for just a headache. It could be so much worse than that." I was wrong.

On Thanksgiving morning, Stephanie and I prepared dishes for the family gathering. The phone rang as I took that spectacular sweet potato casserole out of the oven.

That was in the day when phones still existed on the walls and tables of our homes. The kitchen phone had an impressively long, coiled cable. As I cradled the yellow plastic receiver to my face, I was about to experience the next time I heard my dad cry.

"They've called code blue... I don't know what's going on...

doctors are coming from everywhere… Son, we need to pray…"

Stephanie and I raced to the car. I was amazed that even as I drove nearly 90 miles an hour down the interstate in a rush to get to the hospital, cars still passed me. "Oh, are you on the way to your dying mother, too?" I cynically wondered.

That morning, the specialist quizzed mom about the mundane things one asks when checking on mental acuity. "Do you know what year this is?" "Who is the president?" "Who is this person here with you in your room?"

Though mom's headaches had mercilessly left her dazed for days, she and dad were able to have a clear, happy conversation that morning. But as the doctor was going through his tests, she looked to dad, with a tear rolling down her cheek, and said, "I never knew it would be…"

It would be what? Today? This hard? The end? There was no end to the sentence. Caught in the middle of a thought, she was gone. Her body held on til the following Monday, but I'm convinced she left us at that moment. It turns out that the cancer in her liver was far worse than the doctors realized. A deadly combination of a failing liver and blood thinner medication led to a massive stroke.

At her funeral, one of her dear friends put on a brave face and sang *It Is Well With My Soul*.

Looking deep into his face, I said, "Dad, I feel like I should cancel the wedding. I mean, I wonder if I need to stay here at home with you." I've always been prone to making quick, rash pronouncements like this.

"Son, don't you do that for a moment. I'll be fine. You'll be fine.

I'm so proud of you, son." Richard Fish was such a good man.

———————

The last time I heard my dad cry was on December 28, 1989.

That was the day before my wedding as I busily gathered and packed the last of my things to move to Barbara's apartment. Dad was in the hallway, looking on with tears rolling down his face.

It wasn't quite a thousand-year hug, but I still remember dad's powerful arms holding me tightly as we both sobbed. Just a month after mom's exit, I was also leaving the house. It was a beautiful, painful moment.

The next day, dad stood next to me as my best man. Barbara and I began a life together as man and wife.

———————

Here's something interesting to note, though I'm not sure it has any meaning beyond my sentimentality. Dad and mom had been married for 25 years, and dad was 50 when mom died. After 25 years of marriage, as I neared my fiftieth birthday, Barbara died from the long-term results of a life spent battling rheumatoid arthritis.

I wish dad could have been there with me that day when Barbara slipped away. But then, maybe he was. My father wrapped me in his strong arms of love every time he showed me what it meant to walk with a wife that was dying. He had knitted words of hope into me with every word of encouragement he gave me. I survived my mother's early death and had the strength to walk through the loss of my young wife because dad's goodness was faithful, dependable, and reliable.

I have walked through grief, I have stumbled and nearly fallen, but I have never lost the battle. I wonder if it's something unique inside me because I'm Richard's son.

22

- Away -

With a stout jerk and little thought, dad yanked the blanket from the back of the moving van and gave it a fling. But inside the wrap was a treasure; an irreplaceable sheet of milk glass that sat on the ledge of an antique dental cabinet, a family heirloom.

The milk glass flew out of the blanket and spun through the air in an impressive slow-motion manner. The men of the first church I was about to pastor had gathered to help with the move. They pointed and gasped as the few seconds of air-bound travel time seemed to linger for minutes. Finally, the irreplaceable piece landed on the ground, breaking into pieces.

Just hours earlier, dad had packed that milk glass carefully, circumspectly, in the protective blanket with a stern lecture on how I should take great care as I stowed such items.

I wanted to laugh and cry all at the same time.

Several years after my mother's death, a call came that I had expected. As dad began the conversation, he was doing something he would have labeled as hem-hawing. So often, he would rigidly tell me to stop hem-hawing and "Spit it out." That day, dad was fully engaged in the ol' hem-haw maneuver.

Finally, he got to the point, one that his hesitant words foreshadowed. "Son, I'd like to ask Sharon to marry me. I just, well, I guess, I, uh, I wanted to make sure you were OK with that."

Let's rewind just a bit.

From mom's hospital bed, as the reality of her cancer was drilling deep into her spirit, she decided it was time to prepare me for what was to come.

"Now, someday, your dad will want to marry again. And I know exactly who he's gonna marry," she instructed me in the same manner a teacher would speak to their student.

"Who's that?" I asked with my face in full scrunch mode.

"He's going to marry Arnetta. You just watch. I know he will."

I didn't want to even think about such a thing.

She continued, "And when he calls you and asks you if you mind if he marries Arnetta, you support him in every way. I've seen families torn apart when a parent remarries. You support him. Let him be happy."

Now back to the hem-hawing phone call.

"Son, I want to marry Sharon. How would you feel about that?" dad asked.

I had long realized that dad had no interest in marrying Arnetta. She was a dear friend, even a second mother to me when mom died. But there was no attraction between the two.

How, then, did I feel about dad remarrying? Would I be a help or a hindrance in the process? Could I allow him to be happy and whole again, even in the shadow of my grief over losing mom at a young age?

Standing in the kitchen of the first house I ever owned, I gladly and happily gave my endorsement. "If you wanna marry her, I'll support you 100%."

Mom wanted that, even if she didn't get to pick his match. That's what my character demanded of me, and it is what love does at a time like this.

———

In 2000, I transitioned from a career in radio to full-time pastoral ministry. Over the next two decades, I would serve as pastor at four different churches, and dad and Sharon were on hand for the first three moves.

You only realize how much stuff you own once you pack it for a move. And I've had to do that repeatedly, each time ridding myself of more and more possessions, trying to ease the load. Looking back, I wonder if dad would have made a great professional mover. His ability to fit pieces of life together in a truck, like stacking wood in a rick, was without rival. And except for the milk glass incident when, without thinking, he flung one of the most irreplaceable pieces on the truck to its demise, he had an intuitive sense about stacking, packing, supporting, and unloading possessions for maximum efficiency.

———

I often wonder what would have changed if I had stayed closer to home. I wonder what would have changed if I'd pursued my dream of working in Nashville, Tennessee. I wonder what would have changed if I could have fished more, walked more, and talked more with dad. But beautiful relationships have a permanence that time and distance can't destroy. I had a calling to pursue, and dad was always with me, even if not physically. The seismic shift of my life could not alter the history of two men inextricably bound as father and son. And more than that, I could live by the character and values built with the watchful eye of a good earthly father.

No distance could change the man I am because I'm Richard's son.

23

- The Bad Guy -

Every story worth telling has a protagonist. A bad guy. A villain. Someone we love to boo and hiss.

At the end of the story, if all ends are tied, and all corners tucked, the protagonist gets his comeuppance. It's Die Hard's Hans Gruber and his fall at Nakatomi Plaza. It's Back To The Future's Biff and the poo truck. It's Thanos disintegrating into dust at the snap of an Avenger.

But in real life, the bad guy sometimes wins. And bad guys tend to come more nuanced; they are deeply loved and even revered by those in their inner circle. Measuring the badness of a real-life character can be as dubious as measuring greatness.

To understand Richard Fish, you must also appreciate his willingness to go above and beyond for the most questionable of individuals. The fact that he befriended a narcissistic con artist, and maintained a level of affection and openness towards this individual, might cause you to suspect that dad was gullible. Dad knew that this man named Judas was taking advantage of his kind heart. That's not the protagonist's real name, of course, and not the least bit artistically subtle. But it will do.

Judas was the type of individual who spoke in put-downs. There was always a snarl and innuendo, even if enigmatically wrapped in words of greeting. He was the type of man who highly valued his image. In buying expensive things, he would posit that he was a man of refined tastes, unlike others. In relationships, he was most concerned about what was in it for him.

In other words, this man was the polar opposite of dad. And dad loved him with a rare grace.

Once, while dad was licking his wounds over being taken advantage of again, I asked him why he tolerated this person. Dad admitted that casting Judas aside would be the wise thing to do. However, he told me that he felt God had called him to positively influence a person who likely had few other good role models.

Judas conned dad out of a small fortune. Dad wanted to make a difference for good in this man's life. But in the end, Judas basked in how much he was able to take from dad. He even once smugly hissed to my sister, "I was the only one who really cared about your dad."

In a good movie, she would have punched his lights out.

In real life, the shock so reverberated through her system she was speechless.

Judas walked away with his treasure. What is the nature of grace when applied to people like this? Will he ever reach a point of soul-reckoning that brings him to repentance and restitution? That day has not yet come.

I want to struggle with you for a moment when considering what we do with people like this when they unceremoniously enter our stories.

Just as dad would not dismiss Judas, I cannot dismiss him either. As much as I want to refer to him as loathsome and treacherous, I'm also aware that dad saw elements of good in him. Perhaps I can understand this fiber of dad's character because I sometimes find it in myself. It's this tiny splinter of hope that all men are amenable to being redeemed. It's this notion that God seems to faithfully love us and grace our lives even when dotted with the most reckless abandon.

"Dad, I just don't get why you let him get away with taking advantage of you," I bemoaned.

"Son, he's not taking advantage of me. I know exactly what he's doing." Dad was quick with that reply.

"Then, why? Why let him?"

Deep sigh. "I may be the only person in this world other than his family who shows kindness to him. How's he gonna know who God is if no one bothers to show him kindness?"

"Alright… but it hurts to see him do these things to you." I wanted so desperately to fix things. But I couldn't just take the problem apart, determine what had gone awry, mend it, then put it back together again.

Dad had a way of reframing difficulties in spiritual terms. "Well, I reckon that I've put a whole lot more hurt on Christ than any person has ever put on me. If Jesus can love me anyway, I 'spose I can love Judas anyway."

"You're a better man than me," I said.

"Son, you're fine. You're fine. Just some things we got to do that don't always look right by what the world thinks we should do." Dad was right, of course.

I have learned that there are times in life when we must walk away from toxic people. But I also struggle with the fact that dad lived an allegiance to hurting people even as those people were putting their hurt back on him.

"Remember me in the light of your unfailing love, for you are merciful, O Lord." (Psalm 25:7b, NLT)

There are plenty of things in me that are unlovable. My faults might seem overwhelming to those who only know me from a distance. That's why there is something perplexingly refreshing about the absolute goodness of God's grace and mercy. Somebody loves us and sees us as redeemable. Somebody deals grace to our treachery and mercy to our deceit. Somebody who knows us inside and out chooses to love us inside and out.

So as I try to find my way through this life, I've decided that I should try to wear this ethic as my own. I should try to muster up love for someone who otherwise might be discarded and lost. It's a principle that confounds the wise but is sealed up in my soul because I'm Richard's son.

ANOTHER ALL-TIME FAVORITE OF MINE.

DAD, WITH GRANDSON KYLE.

24

- The Phone Call -

Red eyes and a volcanic flow of snot and tears are not a public speaker's friend. It messes with your senses and probably presents far too many unanswerable questions to those who come to listen to what you have to say.

As I pressed that flat, glass-cold iPhone to the side of my face on that early Sunday morning, I took a deep breath reminding myself that I'd better not let these high emotions get the best of me. I had a congregation to tend to. I had a message to bring on that Sabbath day.

High emotions were, at that moment, living large in my chest. Like the steam rising from those foothills of the Allegheny where I lived, I was fairly certain that my anxiety was about to spring out of me and rise in great visual display for all to see.

For many months, I had been absorbing the realities of dad's cancer. Pancreatic cancer, to be more specific. As that insipid disease wore away his body, it caverned a deep dark hole into my spirit.

I was serving as pastor at a church in a beautiful region near the place where the Ohio river carved a ridge between the Buckeye State and West Virginia. Getting back to southern Indiana required six long hours of travel time. Not to mention that my wife, Barbara, was struggling with a life-threatening illness. Six long hours, and a wife with health issues, made regular visits difficult. That meant that every time I could go, cancer had broken dad down even more. Just when I thought he couldn't lose any more weight, his formerly solid, muscular frame would appear even more fragile.

———

In the hours before the congregation would arrive at the church that Sunday morning, I paced the floor of that spacious office, praying but mostly telling God what he ought to think about this mess.

Finally, I had reached an epiphany. Without consulting Barbara or asking God what he thought of the idea, I decided to leave the church and go back home to help care for dad. Never mind that I had no idea what I would do for a job. Those pesky little gnat-like thoughts couldn't be bothered with at a time like this.

Somehow I just knew dad would answer the phone. And, as always, he sounded glad to hear from me. After a few moments of small talk, I took a deep breath and opened my heart to dad.

"You're not doing well, and I feel so guilty about being so far away. I've decided to quit so I can come home and be with you."

———

Throughout my growing-up years, dad would proclaim that he would work me like a barred mule. At least, that's what I thought he was saying. In my mind, I pictured the poor, over-worked mule attached to some wooden beam, pulling a cart as a leather strop whipped into his back. In recent years I've revisited this colloquial saying of dad's and realized I was only hearing his country-boy pronunciation. What he was telling me was I was about to be worked like a BORROWED mule. The implication is that something borrowed is treated more harshly than something owned.

There was nothing violent about dad's intent at all. His sense of humor escaped me at the time. My dad was the hardest-working man I've ever known, and he knew that the younger version of me could never work with the same vigor or passion that he applied. But be certain, be very certain, I would encounter hard work. I thought I was being driven like a barred mule. It turns out I was learning the value of hard work.

Another misperception that has been peeled away by age is the one that kept me from seeing dad as my protector and defender. Introducing me to hard work was a form of protecting me from the ravages of the laziness. This man, who seemed like a ruthless taskmaster, was my advocate. He looked out for me.

It's no wonder that when the moment arrived, my very nature cried out for me to look out for dad. The intrinsic lesson he peppered into my soul was that one of the main jobs of life is to work hard at looking after each other. Maybe that meant we spent hours working in the garden. Maybe that meant grunting as we chopped wood for winter fires. Maybe it meant we went the extra mile for someone in need. That ethic has been etched onto my bones, and the etching could be a bit painful at times.

The pain of my tears in contemplating dad's death, and the pain of feeling like I was contributing so little of value to dad's last days, drove me to work harder. I needed to take up the challenging task. Put my back into it. Let the sweat pour from my brow. There was hard work to be done, and doing it now came naturally.

Now, about that phone call.

I took a deep breath—a holy pause. Then, I got to the reason I called.

"You're not doing so well, and I feel so guilty being so far away. I've decided to quit so I can come home and be with you."

In the hours before I was to lead worship as pastor of BeginningPointe Church, my anxiety over dad's battle with pancreatic cancer was peaking. Miles away from him, in that idyllic little hamlet, the distance from home also served as a measuring stick for my distress at being away.

I was confident that the only option left was to leave the ministry and return to Columbus, Indiana, to help care for dad.

———

Dad had been called into pastoral ministry, and it was one of the aching regrets of his life that he failed to go. Don't get me wrong; there are many ways to minister the love and Good News of Jesus into the world. But the call to be a pastor is a rare, unique thing essential to taking leadership of a church. Dad had that call.

As a young believer, fresh out of the military and gleaming with Spirit-infused potential, dad was invited to serve as an associate pastor by a well-regarded minister. Dad couldn't clearly explain why he passed on the opportunity.

In subsequent years, he proved to be a powerful presence in the Columbus, Indiana, Free Methodist Church as a layman. He was loved as a teacher, leader, and occasional speaker. There was a certain country-boy charm to dad's sincere, genuine way of explaining Scripture. Though he was never schooled in exegesis or homiletics, he spent hours reading commentaries and books on theology. His seminary was the humble green vinyl-and-duct-tape recliner where he perched by the hot stove to study late into the evening after a hard day.

Following mom's death, there was a point at which dad once again weighed the possibility of diving fully into some sort of ministry. This time, he contemplated missionary work. Once again, he sat aside the calling.

But isn't it amazing how God can still use us in our reluctance to obey? Dad may not have served as a minister of God on foreign soil, but he was undoubtedly a firebrand evangelist wherever he set his feet. And God blessed that work.

Then, there was the calling that fell upon his son. That would be me.

Have you ever watched a sporting event where an athlete had just accomplished a mind-blowing fete, and a reporter sticks a mic into the face of a glowing father who shines with pride for his offspring? I suspect you would have seen a similar reaction from dad had there been interest from any of the major networks when I finally said yes to my calling into pastoral ministry.

In the weeks before I accepted the leadership mantle at my first church, dad gleefully bought me a new suit. He was clothing me with his enthusiastic approval. The suit would symbolize dad's presence with me as I went forward into the arduous task of the pastorate. It's still nestled in my closet.

From that point forward, for the remainder of his life, whenever there was a move to be made to a new church, dad would be there helping me pack, load, move, unload, unpack, and settle in. He would survey a new parsonage and declare without fail, even when it may have been an overstatement, "Son, this is a fine place to live. A fine place."

Dad would visit my churches and loved building relationships with my congregations. "Son, these are mighty fine people. Mighty fine."

And when he would hear me deliver a sermon, his praise and encouragement were never sparse. "That was a fine sermon, son. Fine sermon."

Even when we disagreed about my ministry approach, there was no mistaking his pride in my work. Once, as I prepared to lead a congregation through a radical course of action, dad cautioned me. "Son, I'm not sure you ought to do that. We old people don't like change." I would smile and pat his arm. With a deep sigh, he affirmed that he would pray and support me even though he didn't like the direction. After all, he knew I was following the Holy Spirit as best as I could. He would eventually draw in a deep breath and nod his head. "You'll do fine, son. You'll do fine."

I believe that dad was living vicariously through me in those days. I am a part of Richard Fish; I walk and breathe and speak and teach and reach out with a body made of strong stock. Even now, as dad is gone from this earth, I sense his presence in my work. I do very few things that I don't eventually realize that I am my father's son.

My work as a pastor is an integral part of who I have been in this life, and it's also something that made my dad incredibly proud. Dad may not have said yes to being a full-time pastor, but he went into the ministry with me.

There was no reluctance or hesitation in me at all. I would have left the pastoral ministry right at the moment of that phone call in late 2012 and gone to dad's side. Yet I failed to realize how I had never actually left his side.

"I'll come home and be with you." That was my message to my dying father.

The words he said next are forged into my soul like steel. They are words that were so monumental I suspect God himself breathed them directly into dad's spirit as he delivered his response.

"Oh, son," dad sighed. "You're doing exactly what God called you to do. And I've never felt closer to you in my life."

It was an anointing. It was a blessing. It was a charge and a commission. It was to be a keystone moment.

To have left the ministry would have been tantamount to dad himself walking away from God. There was to be no turning away from what God called me to do. Dad and I were always together through those days, even when we were distant.

And today, as my ministry work has taken different forms and functions, I still feel that presence with me just as sure as God Himself has constantly been abiding.

———————

"Richard, where is Greg?" someone might have asked him in those last months. "Where has your son been?"

"Oh, he isn't here right now," he could have replied. "But I've been with him. Every day. Every second."

In the same way, we are never too far away to experience the full power of God's love in our lives. I love that line from Psalm 25 that says, "He (God) shows the proper path to those who go astray." While I wasn't astray from God, my logic had failed me when I decided to leave the ministry to care for dad. The correction I received was the reminder that because I was following closely to the calling of God, my dad felt closer to me than ever. I remind myself of that often. God shows me the right path when my thinking goes off-center, or my logic fails me. He reminds me that He is with me.

Without God's divine and empowering presence, I could not do the things I've been called to do.

Dad's words to me on the day of the phone call still reverberate in my heart and mind. They were formative words, instructive words, and life-changing words. They came in a moment that both summed up my history and future in one tidy phrase; a combination of words no doubt breathed full of God's Holy guidance. I was doing what God had called me to do, and dad felt closer to me than ever.

As I walk this pathway with the memories of dad once again, I am renewed and strengthened for whatever the final decades of my journey bring. I can find my way forward. I remember dad's loving ways that I once interpreted as tyrannical, and I find what I need to trudge on through whatever challenges may come.

I am enriched, empowered, and enlivened because I'm Richard's son.

ONE OF THE **LAST PICTURES** I EVER TOOK OF **DAD**. HE GOT COLD A LOT IN THOSE DAYS, SO BARBARA MADE HIM AN AFGHAN. DAD LOVED IT.

25

– The Old Man –

There are nights when I lay in bed, unable to sleep, and I open my eyes to stare into the pitch black dark.

If the curtain hasn't been closed perfectly tight, the faintest wisp of light cuts in. Because my eyes have become accustomed to the dark, even the smallest degree of light can make outlines in the room visible to my eyes. It's awesome that even the sparse light of night, even the gentle glow of the moon, can be enough to break through the hollow emptiness of the early hours. Then, I soak in the moment, allowing God to drench me to the core with His presence.

Darkness can never defeat the light. And there are times in the dark cave of total emptiness when you can take advantage of the deep, surrounding darkness to recognize the still, small glow.

The old man sitting on the couch next to me hunched over his cane, dancing in and out of lucidity. At times, a stream of saliva fell from his mouth. As if waking from a weird dream, he'd pull his hanky out and wipe the spit away, surprised that it was there.

Those solid muscular shoulders were replaced by pointed bones, his sweater a landscape of sharp hills and valleys. "Hey, son," he'd say, realizing I was there, my hand gently rubbing his back.

He took a frail breath and said, "You know, I looked in the mirror and didn't recognize the man I saw. I asked myself, 'Who is that old man?'"

All I could do was listen and strain to hold back the tears. But then I'd break in with the most important words I could say, words that needed to be heard again, "I love you, dad."

"I love you too, son."

There are a hundred thousand things I wish I'd said and a hundred thousand more questions I wished I'd asked. But then, our life had been so full, so rich, so complete, it seemed that few words needed to be given air. These were sacred moments, moments that would last a thousand years.

Here was the man who carried me out into the hallway of the trailer where we lived when I was a baby. The little hat on my head fell off and rolled down the hallway as my mother screamed, "Richard! His head fell off!" I can only imagine the sly smirk on dad's face as he drank in the moment.

Here was the man who would lay next to me on an air mattress in a two-man pup tent on a fishing trip at Lake Monroe, Indiana. The trot lines had been set, and a ten-pound catfish awaited us the next day. But that night, as we drifted off to sleep, dad's voice rang out in prayer. "Heavenly Father, I thank you for this beautiful day you've given me with my son, Gregory...."

Here was the man who swatted my bottom the day I punched my sister in the face. As I swung away, I thought she would move. We'd played that game so many times before. I'd say, "I'm gonna close my eyes and swing my fist, and you'd better move." That day, with friends nearby, she decided to take one, I suppose, to glory in my fall. Truthfully, though, the punch might as well have gone straight to my face, and I was willing to take the swat on the bottom for my horrible game gone awry.

Here was the man who would torment us in the van when he'd pull out his harmonica to play. He'd blow the reed quickly from one side to the next, then begin to puff away a tune. "Dad! Would you put that away?!"

Here was the man who wanted to share his love of the book of Revelations with his kids, not realizing I was utterly terrified by the imagery. There would be nights I could see an orangish harvest moon and think it was running red with blood. I'd pull the covers up and pray, "Jesus, please don't come tonight. Please don't come tonight." I would listen for a trumpet or the rumble of horsemen as carefully as a child listens for reindeer hooves at Christmas. He wanted us to enjoy thinking about the end times like he did, but it only scared young Greg.

Yes, sitting next to me on that blue couch was an old man that even I hardly recognized. An old man that I knew to the bone.

There, by his side, I made dad a promise that seemed to bring happiness to his spirit.

"Dad, I've never been a shoutin' Christian like you," I began.

Dad wasn't concerned about what others thought. When he was blessed with a special understanding of the presence of God, he would shout in joy.

"Dad, I've never been a shouter," I said plaintively, "But when I know that you finally see Jesus face to face, I'll shout with you. You shout in Glory, I'll shout here."

He nodded in agreement.

We prayed for a miracle, and I believe we got one. Dad lasted longer in his fight against pancreatic cancer than anyone could have imagined. Maybe it was out of pure Richard Fish bullheadedness, but death wasn't about to push my dad around.

The day came when dad was so emaciated, he looked like those pictures of concentration camp victims I had been shown in high school history class.

In early 2013, we were called back to Columbus, Indiana. Dad was fading fast. Those may have been his last days, but they were full of strange wonders.

In the rare moments that dad spoke, he was mostly confused. He was convinced he needed to get out of bed and take on some mysterious task. Even in dying, dad wanted to be active.

Many family members gathered around him, keeping vigil. Others came and went. One morning as I walked into his room, his wife Sharon said, "Hey Richard, Greg's here!"

One final time, dad spoke to me. He opened his eyes, and for a few seconds, dad was himself. He smiled and said, "Well, hey, son!"

And then he faded off.

I will never forget those beautiful final words to me. Perhaps capping off a lifetime of thousands and thousands of times where he called me son, there was one more. And it was perfect.

Later that day, dad opened his eyes, looked into the distance, and said, "Hey, hon!" Others in the room were confused. "Who's he talking to?" they wondered. "Who's Don?"

But my sister and I understood what he was saying. "Hey, hon.

Yeah, I know. I'll see you in a little while." He was Sharon's husband, no doubt about that. But somewhere in his mind, he saw mom standing at the edge of Heaven, perhaps, taking the edge off of the transition he was about to make. I don't understand the mysteries of marriage, remarriage, and the heavenly ramifications. But I'm OK with that.

Speaking of uncertain theologies, I'm not sure what to make of this next part, either. I hear stories of people that have seemed to wait until they were alone in a room to slip away. I'm not sure we have much control over those final moments. But still, some think it's not uncommon for us to wait until we are alone to die.

That evening of dad's homegoing, Stephanie was exhausted and went to take a nap. I had left the room to eat a sandwich. The sun was beginning to set. That was when they came to tell us that he was gone.

As the family gathered at his side, I didn't dare wait. I knew at that moment that dad was experiencing the death of faith and the birth of sight. He was finally face to face with his life's greatest hope; dad was crossing Jordan and running to embrace Christ. He was shouting happy. I just knew it. And so, I got shouting happy for him and let out the biggest whoop of my life.

I'm not sure that others in the family were all that pleased with me. As they cried, I let 'er rip. You're not supposed to get shouting happy when someone dies. But I did... I whooped. Just as I had promised, I joined dad in his exuberant cry.

There are moments when I step beyond myself and my conventions because of a divine bond. A divine bond that attaches me to the heart of someone I love and draws me to do new things, to taste new experiences. Dad's death wasn't so much a dying as it was a glorious crossing over. And it was my joy to mark the moment with him. No Kleenex and tears for me at that moment. Nope. I shouted royally. I did it because I'm Richard's son.

26

- *Running In Heaven* -

Dad had a rabid hunger for Heaven. He had already tasted a sampling of Heaven and had his appetite whetted.

Perhaps I should let dad tell you about it himself. Here's the story I pulled together from dad's words.

"Running shoes on, muscles stretched, I was ready to forget the day's stress with a peaceful run on a beautiful summer evening. The bright moon on a clear night made it seem almost like day.

"I had come to youth camp to teach woodcraft to 120 high-energy campers. The project involved several pieces of wood and a lot of hammering. Multiply that times 60 campers in each session, plus a barrage of questions coming all at once, and you have quite an adventure on your hands. It made little difference that I had two helpers; pieces were still assembled upside down and backward. Each evening was spent endlessly making corrections. By the time I finished up on this particular night, chapel was already over. So, I decided to go for a run.

"As I set out, I dedicated the five miles to praising God. With each stride, I lavished every word of adoration that came to my mind. Recalling the Psalms, I glorified, magnified, heaped majesty, exalted His Name, and praised His holiness, might, and faithfulness. Every breath was breathed in praise of God.

"It was already a beautiful night, but it seemed that every word of honor to God made it even lovelier. Every passing moment ushered me into an event that was to be more incredible and indescribable than I'd ever thought it could be. I've always imagined that every child of God had experiences like this. But as I grow older, I've come to believe this was a rare and sacred event.

"As I lifted glory to God with all that was within me, I began to run effortlessly. It was almost as if I was floating. I'd never ran with that sort of ease before, nor have I since. I was so close to God that I felt only a step away from Heaven. I experienced such elated joy I hoped it would never stop. I knew I was more in the presence of God than I'd ever been before. Words are inadequate to describe it.

"And then, I became aware of something else.

"With each deep breath in, I noticed a very sweet fragrance around me. The run became saturated with the rich smell of honeysuckle.

"To my utter amazement, a later run in the daylight revealed no honeysuckle along that route. I have since heard of great revivals where a very sweet fragrance settled in with the presence of the Holy Spirit. It struck me immediately that what I smelled was the very presence of God.

"Every time I recall that night, I long to be in God's presence that way again. I have a great family and a wonderful life. However, I can easily say that my heart longs for the day when I step across that river dividing Heaven from this life and stand directly in the presence of my Savior.

"Such an encounter with God is something that no one should ever miss. At the end of the day, full of trouble and tension, my path is set. The course is laid out before me. I will run into the very presence of God and live with Him forever. I'd love for you to come with me."

I, too, have had unique encounters that remind me of the realness, the closeness, the faithfulness, and the wonder of the presence of God.

Maybe all those stories from the book of Revelations needed to be implanted into my young mind so that I won't be afraid as I approach the dawning of my late years in life. Things may get weird. Things may get buggy. Things may get scary. But eventually, in the last chapter, the God who holds all things together will bring it all together for the good of those who follow Him.

I had asked dad if it would be alright for me to preach his funeral. Beloved pastor Mel Nead would give a beautiful homily that day, but in the end, I wanted to stand as testimony to this man and the legacy he left. I prepared well for that moment when I would rise and speak to the house packed with hundreds of people.

Standing before them, I looked at my notes and saw nothing but a blur. The message I had labored over now looked like hieroglyphics. So instead of sharing what I had brought, I took a deep breath and let the Holy Spirit speak through me. I can't brag about myself or what happened at that moment. I can only brag about a God who had something even better to say. I just had the privilege of being the instrument He used.

I'm not some great spiritual profit. I'm just a man. I'm just an earthbound soul discovering goodness where I can. I learned that from dad. Dad, full of flaws and rough places, changed many people's lives.

For hours and hours at the wake, I heard stories about how dad took the time for those who needed him. I heard about fishing trips he'd hosted. Amazingly, those who went with dad never talked about the fish they caught. It was always about the time they spent with Richard Fish.

"Son, your daddy was a great man," some would say.

I would smile and thank them, but in my heart, I knew he was something better. He was good.

I know that for a fact because I'm Richard's son.

27

– The Day Dad and Grandpa Carried Me to the Hospital –

A crushing pain began to sweep across my abdomen in the early hours of a chilly March morning.

I was in my mid-fifties, living alone and far from family. When an emergency happens, it's difficult to decide who is best to call. So, I decided to tough it out.

As the pain increased, I paced the floor, sure that it would eventually relent. It did not. I felt sick as if the flu had suddenly knitted itself into my body. I cried out in prayer that God would rescue me. He did.

It was as if Grandpa Glen Fish was saying, "There's something wrong with this boy. We need to get him to a doctor now."

Dad would get frustrated if I brought home a bad grade. For me, a bad grade was a C. I was capable of A work, but I was lazy with my studies. He would challenge me, but he would always end by quietly admitting he was not a good student. In fact, he wondered if he'd make it to graduation day, and he nearly didn't, but for entirely different reasons.

Weeks before commencement at the 1950s version of Columbus High School, dad was sick and getting sicker. All the symptoms pointed to the flu. Dad had never felt worse in his young life. As the days progressed, he couldn't eat, he couldn't go to school, and he couldn't run with the guys. He could only lay around the house, groaning, doubled over in pain.

After a day of work at Arvin's, Grandpa Fish came home to see his son still bent over in pain after days of misery. "There's something wrong with this boy," he said in anguished tones. "We need to get him to a doctor now."

The diagnosis came quickly. Appendicitis. Surgery was needed immediately, and it would be the early version of an appendectomy, where a large incision was made in the side of the abdomen. The recuperation time was long and grueling.

If one more day had passed before seeking help, you likely would not be reading this book now. Thousands of fish might have remained free to explore their fishly pursuits. Florence Foster might have married a man named Ed or Ray or Ronald. It's a kick in the gut to think of how this world would be different if they had waited one more day.

———————

I had been having occasional bursts of pain on Monday, but they seemed normal and reasonably explainable.

By Tuesday morning's early hours, I knew something more severe was at play. I was no stranger to gut pains, as one of my doctors used to call them, and I now understand why dad took those so seriously.

At the age of 12, I would be in the throws of some horrific intestinal pain. As soon as dad found out about it, he left work to take me to the hospital. We discovered that my issues were irritable bowel syndrome. For a number of years, I had to monitor my diet carefully and take medication.

My stomach issues eventually lightened up.

But this was no irritated bowel. It was something strangely more powerful and unrelenting. It was still early in the morning, and I did not want to wake up my friends asking for a ride to the emergency room. So, I waited. And the pain grew worse.

I can't tell you that I have a strong theology about how, possibly, the presence of our loved ones can sneak into our lives long after they are gone. All I can say is that morning, as I tried to talk myself out of seeking help, dad came home from work early and swept me up in his arms. Grandpa Fish saw me in my pain and declared that it was time to move for help.

Somehow, I managed to drive myself to the hospital. (I'm sure the lawyers will want me to tell you not to do this yourself; always call an ambulance, and don't be like me.) Truly though, if such things can happen, my dad and my grandpa were really in control of the car - they were the ones who helped me walk when I could barely move. Their mysterious presence helped me find my way into an emergency room, where I collapsed onto a cold hospital bed with thin white sheets.

There were flurries of activity in my room, punctuated by moments of dark silence. Though I was floating on a cloud of morphine, I understood every word the surgeon said as he told me I was experiencing appendicitis and would soon be having my appendix removed. The modern procedure is much kinder to the body, with three small puncture holes placed for most operations. They called it a Lappy Appy (for Laparoscopic Appendectomy).

As the surgeon stood at the foot of my bed the next day, he let me know I wasn't out of the woods yet. The appendix had ruptured, and bile leaked into my abdomen. If I had waited much longer to get to the hospital, you wouldn't be reading this chapter now. There seems to be a familiar ring to that line.

Over the days ahead, my body fought hard. Richard Fish hard. And after three days, I was free to go home. Something feels rather miraculous about that.

As I write this chapter, still nursing the painful wounds, my clearness of mind is returning, and the pain is becoming more manageable. But somehow, once again, I feel strangely connected to my dad. And grandpa. There's something perfectly wonderful about having a good father. It has given me a clearer picture of the good Heavenly Father I have. I understand new things about provision, paying attention, doing right things, and finding peace.

Father, SHOW ME the way…

LEAD ME, and I will follow…

REMEMBER your unfailing love…

FORGET my failure…

My hope is in you.

I cannot forget who I am. I always seem to find my bearings because I'm Richard's son.

And because we have a loving Father God, we can SURVIVE and even THRIVE. We can find our way forward. We're not too lost or too far off the path. Times aren't so bad, and circumstances so dire that we can't find a way forward.

Through Jesus, God showed us the path to follow.

Through Jesus, He leads us.

Through Jesus, God remembers his compassion for us.

And, through Jesus, He made it possible to forget our stinky moments.

God welcomed me in and called me a son. Richard Fish would want me to remind you that God would love to call you son or daughter.

If you are struggling to pray, or just need fresh words to say, pray this prayer with me one more time:

Father, SHOW ME the way…

LEAD ME, and I will follow…

REMEMBER your unfailing love…

FORGET my failure…

My hope is in you.

Whether or not we ever attain any measure of greatness is beside the point. We can experience goodness.

I am so thankful for the example of a good man. I'm so grateful for the days in his careful, watchful gaze. I'm also thankful that I can know the Father in Heaven; I learned it to be so because I'm Richard's son.

RICHARD'S SON, WALKING A TRAIL

AT LAKE WORTH, TEXAS.

epilogue
- All the Man -

In the year 2022, I began a new life adventure.

I once would have been happy to spend the full of my days in Southern Indiana. But now, closer to my retirement years than my college days, I find myself hundreds of miles away from the east fork of White River.

Fort Worth, Texas, was a new start. A new marriage, a new job, and a new dream for life.

Here in this dusty, drought-stricken, sultry hot land, I began to walk for exercise again. I even dared to run at times. And as I ran, dad was there with me.

I would pray just as dad did when we ran together back in the late '80s. I'd often smell the honeysuckle along the pathway and feel like I was traveling Heaven's pathways with dad. I could hear his voice encouraging me onward. "Hey, son, you're doing fine. I feel so close to you still. You're gonna make it."

As I walked along Lake Worth's edge, I again decided to lay it on and gear up into a full-speed run. Several steps into the run, as I prayed, as I felt dad keeping step, my knee snapped, crackled, popped, and screamed out in sounds that I'm certain would have translated as profanity.

I slowed back down to a walk as discouragement swirled through my soul.

Though my spirit was willing, my knees were weak. Running was more than they would allow. There were no more wings on my feet.

"Ugh, sorry, dad. If only I could be half the man you were."

There have been moments when I heard God's voice as if someone next to me was speaking. This was to be one of those sacred occassions.

Everything stopped. The whole earth seemingly focused down to that spot on the trail where I walked. Heaven and nature came to a hush as the One who created it all spoke life to me.

"You're not half the man your daddy was. Greg, you're ALL the man I made you to be." That's what the voice said.

And then... life resumed. God grew silent in my spirit, and I walked.

The water lapped against the shoreline, the sun's yellow, dry heat radiated from the cement, and traffic resumed on the nearby road. Life continued.

I drew in a breath of contentment, realizing that greatness was never the goal, let alone matching my dad deed for deed. No, I had Greg-Fish-work to do, and I'm doing good.

I may not be the man my dad was, but that's OK. I can be the man God made me to be, and I can dare to know that good is good enough... because I'm Richard's son.

Some of life's most important, defining moments might be missed altogether if we refuse to press on through the challenges.

Patience doesn't mean we stop in our tracks.

Courage is greater than your biggest boogeyman.

Grumbling has never made a situation better.

Perhaps you're facing something that seems hopeless. It could take the form of a person, a credit report, a bad habit, or a health situation. Maybe you're angry because something has changed and you didn't want it to. Or, you're having relationship issues that have bred bitterness and discontent.

This book will help you discover useful principles that can inhabit your thinking every day, and help you learn to move forward with a new confidence in the One who created you.

There are many books for those who suffer. This book is for those who come along beside someone who suffers. If you are a follower of Jesus, you will eventually find yourself at the side of someone who is hurting. Greg begins with the compelling story of his wife, Barbara, who struggled with a debilitating illness that led to her death in 2015. Remarkably, she did more with her broken body than many of us do with healthy bodies. Sometimes through tears, and sometimes through laughter, you'll find the encouragement and hope you need to walk beside others who are hurting.

Discover God's transformational power to form us into the people we need to be to love and care for the ones we walk with in this life. Each chapter concludes with helpful questions for personal or group study. You'll also receive a short prayer of blessing as you do the hard things that make a difference.

These books, and more, available at
corbinfostermedia.com.

Look for Greg Fish's podcasts from CORBINCAST
on your favorite podcast platform.

CORBIN FOSTER MEDIA

CORBINFOSTER
P U B L I S H I N G

Milton Keynes UK
Ingram Content Group UK Ltd.
UKHW021043181223
434584UK00005B/565